HAUNTED HILL HOUSE

Where Spirits Speak

Martha Hazzard Decker

Gray Fults Press

ISBN- 978-1-7352983-0-1
ISBN-978-1-7352983-1-3

Cover Design by: Teal Gray
Interior Design by: Teal Gray
Cover photo by Martha Hazzard Decker

Printed in the United States of America

This book is dedicated to those who helped dig and discover information and documentation of events at Haunted Hill House. Donna McCauley, your help as a historian has been outstanding. You and Gypsy Jewels who has Zero Discrimination gave me back the desire to dig deep, especially with my metal detector. Katherine and Sonny Estes, without your patience I would never have been able to spend all the time I have in the house alone and with others. Maria Elana Santos Kempf, with your belief that I could do this I have made sure to follow through. Your help with transcribing a very long interview was more than helpful. I appreciate all my friends who have been there with me to explore and experience the house. Deborah Colleen Rose, I appreciate the time we spent discussing the book and your offers to help with whatever I needed. Without the help of Teal Gray, I'm not sure when this story would go to print. You have been ever so helpful. Most of all I would like to thank my husband, Ken, for his patience, belief that I could do this, his support and for all the nights I have spent away from him because I was at the other house. In fact, my truck has traveled the 135 miles to the house so many times the GPS would head to the house when I would tell it to go home.

There is one special friend whom I miss very much I would like to send loving thoughts to through this book. It is in memory of Sheila Gay. She passed this year and is terribly missed in our paranormal community.
Sheila, this book's for you…

CONTENTS

FOREWORD

"Haunted Hill House – Where Spirits Speak" Foreword by Teal Gray

I first met Martha Hazzard Decker over a decade ago. We were both Guest Speakers in her beloved and very haunted town of Jefferson, Texas. This is where we both ultimately meet the owners of Hill house, Katherine and Sonny Estes.

I was impressed by Martha's openness and intelligence from the moment I met her. Her belief in the paranormal was apparent, yet she could keep objectivity, using her keen observation and deductive skills to cut through the unnecessary details and get to the facts. These are traits I admire as a skeptical believer myself. It would be difficult for anyone to put anything over on this paranormal investigator!

Her research has led her to stay many nights in the Haunted Hill House alone. She has told me of the times she was scratched, bitten, growled at, hissed at, watched doors open and close. She heard the piano keys play, heard audible voices, and recorded electronic voice phenomena. She has seen orbs emitting their own light with her own eyes, and yes, I believe her.

I remember talking to Martha once, and we were nowhere near Mineral Wells, but we were talking about the children of Haunted Hill House. Suddenly we look at each other and smile knowingly. The children were with us! We could feel the energy surrounding us as we talked and acknowledged them. We were surrounded by cold spots moving around our legs. Were these the children? We believe it was.

You will find her a guiding presence in this edition of her series on the house, using a unique combination of intellect, intuition, and frankness in every experience presented. She has combined her decades of law enforcement tactics into paranormal investigating. The insight she has into the supernatural world is unique and captures the vibe you feel in the room with the experiencers as they are bitten, scratched, and genuinely terrified.

Moreover, Martha captures the moods and ambiance of the entities, light, and dark. I believe her time investigating the house through the years has made them comfortable to show what they are and were. Secrets are whispered to her, sins revealed. She is forever part of them and Hill House now.

As a bestselling native Texan author and internationally known psychic medium, I cannot imagine a better person than Martha to take you on a journey from the famous East Mountain that sits silently watching over Haunted Hill House. Inside, the Spirits are restless to greet you. Once a makeshift hospital, Bootleggers, prostitutes, card sharks, and outlaws have called Hill House home. Native Americans frequented the caves here, where it is rumored the outlaw Sam Bass hid his gold, and a jewel thief lost his life.
Due to high activity levels, the home has become a world-renowned paranormal site. Take time to sit and deal a hand of cards with the long dead in the Scratcher Room or visit the ghost children in the Carousel Room. You will have an experience you will not forget!

Teal Gray Rev., N.D. is a mysterious sacred site traveler, bestselling native Texas author of nine books. Shades of Angels, Spirited Tales, Haunted Hill House Darkness Resides in Texas, Forget Me Not Memento Mori A World View just to name a few. Check her out at: tealgraybooks.com

Graduate of American Institute of Holistic Theology as a Doctor of Naturology, N.D. and Theological Studies leading to being a doubly ordained Non-Denominational Interfaith Minister.

She has amassed many paranormal and unexplained experiences gaining a greater understanding of the unknown. Sharing that knowledge with you is her passion. Teal has touched many lives with her gifts of prophecy and mediumship throughout the world. Assisting numerous paranormal teams with research of haunted houses, hotels and buildings around the globe.

PREFACE

Greetings fellow readers,

My hope is that you will enjoy this compilation of information about Haunted Hill House. Then be excited to find out more in the upcoming books in this series. Enjoy what you read. Take away from it what you want. Never be afraid to ask questions or dig into the world and its many mysteries. This house is an enigma and a massive puzzle of what, ifs and how. It can lead to deeper thought about many things and touch anyone in different ways. Thanks for taking your time to read about this incredulous house.

One note I did want to make is that there is more than one version of the events which occurred in the house and even in the history. The owners have worked diligently and tirelessly to uncover the truth and to let the history be known to the best of their ability. This is not an entertainment "haunted house." What happens here is real. Hundreds if not thousands of people can attest to their own personal experiences. One of the books in this series well cover all the paranormal activity. This book is only the beginning and I have only touched the surface.

What I will add in the series may be a little of everything, including rumors, myths and folklore in addition to what is documented. Many of the photographs I personally shot. Others have been provided by the owners of the house and others who have granted permission for them to be used. The owners provided a number of documents they received from the previous owner. Some information I found in newspapers, books and online. I will make every effort to give credit for the items when I have the credit information.

Martha Hazzard Decker

WHY I HAD TO WRITE THIS STORY

I met Katherine (Kathy) and Sonny Estes the fall of 2018 thanks to a close friend of all three, Maria Elana Santos Kempf. The Estes' met Kempf during one of their trips to Jefferson, Texas for the paranormal conference, History, Haunts & Legends. Kempf and I have attended for many years. We both are speakers. Kempf is a gifted psychic medium who the Estes' were drawn to for a reading. It's history since then. I was invited to attend an event they were holding in October 2018. Kempf was going as a psychic. The Estes' had vendors outside and were conducting tours through the downstairs of the house. I was there to help out and it was my first time at the house. I have been so many times since then. I feel fortunate I have been able to spend many nights in the house since then. A lot of those times were alone in the house overnight. Those tales will come later.

I received a walk-through of the house and a brief history. It was the history the Estes' received from the prior owner. Over the years they have found much of the history to be different and have been able to update, often with documentation. Kathy asked if I would be the docent in the Scratch Room. I agreed. The rooms were named before they purchased the house, and they left the names the same. Paranormal teams have conducted investigations in the house through the prior owner. She told me the Scratch Room got its name because there had been 75 documented scratches in the room.

I'm one whom tries to go into locations with an open mind. I knew it stood caddy-corner to the Baker Hotel and had been built quite a few years before the hotel, but 75 scratches? I have been around paranormal activity since I was a young child but never somewhere with this amount of activity. I was polite while sort of rolling my eyes in my head but not in reality. Kathy often tells people I came there to debunk and as a skeptic. Actually, I try to keep an open mind while looking for natural causes. Only when all natural possibilities are ruled out do I begin to consider it might be paranormal.

Groups of 6-8 were brought through the house room by room. There were several hundred people touring the house that night. The line was long and wait times were close to an hour. Each room had someone inside to tell history relating to that room and having an assortment of paranormal equipment available for visitors to use. The equipment was different in each room. I can't recall what entity was in the Scratch Room, but I can tell you I saw a couple dozen scratches form on different individuals during that event. Yes, some could have been done by the person with their arm out of sight, but not all of them. I watched several guys hold their arms out where everyone could see and ask to be scratched. We all watched it happen as it happened. This led me to really take an interest in the house. There was a lot of other activity all over the house that night. There were many EVP's, electronic voice phenomenon. This is when something records a voice that no one hears at the time it's recorded. People were touched and some items moved on their own. Besides the scratches that night there was a chair that moved on its own. No one was standing by it or touching it at the time. Everyone in the room heard it move and felt the movement through the floor. The scratch room is fairly small. The walls are the original wood with no covering. There is a false fireplace in the wall and very small closet. It's about half the depth of a normal closet. Some people won't go into the closet and shut the door because at times they can't get back out. The doorknob won't turn. This happened with a tour group. I had to open the door and let the person out. There is a table and chairs in the middle of the room, and it's set up like a poker room.

The more history I learned about the house and the number of murders occurring there drove me to seek out more information. Not only murders but natural death as well. From there it turned into the desire to write a book and compile all this information. I have worked on the book about two years. Finally, I had to say enough. The more we dug, the owners and others, including myself, the more information we found. The book was becoming so big I started to think I would never finish.

With that in mind you are now reading the first book in a series about the house. I'm not sure how many books will come out of the house, but there will be several. This is the first and it is an overview of the house and history. I'll touch lightly on a number of things involving the house. The house has seemed to take on a life of its own. Included is a list of owners, experiences of people and teams at the house, historic information and more. Each of the books will focus on specific details. I'm not sure which comes next.

THE STORY AND HISTORY OF THE HOUSE

Haunted Hill House (HHH) is a 3800 sq. ft. mansion built sometime around or right after the Civil War. It's located at 501 NE 1st St, Mineral Wells, TX. Kathy and Sonny have experienced paranormal activity many times, including when they went to look at the house to see if they wanted to be the next owners. When they were looking at the house to buy, they saw paranormal activity was in the form of a green light. Both saw with their own eyes as it floated down the stairs toward them. They fell in love with the house right then and there. Now they feel that the green orb they watched float down the stairs may have been Jacob. One of the boys murdered in the house. Sonny has formed quite a bond with Joshua and Jacob since then and has strong feeling about how he believes Joshua was treated while he lived in the house. They have opened the house up for individuals and paranormal teams to come for investigations and overnights. Their hope is that someday information will be discovered to help explain and determine the cause for the many layers of activity, good and negative, along with determining if there is a portal, vortex or more in the house or on the property.

The home was a make-shift hospital early 1900s offering healings from the mineral waters. There are two wells on the property which may be two of the first wells in town. Later, during prohibition, it became a brothel and speakeasy, possibly for hotel customers. It was quite the hotel. Many famous people stayed in the hotel hoping to get cured by the mineral waters. There is still talk around town that there are tunnels leading from the hotel to this house and to the church. Talk is that one of the first owners knew Sam Bass. Treasure hunters are still looking for the gold Bass hid. Possibly it's in the caves on the mountain behind the house.

The home once was owned by a family involved in dark occult activity, verified through former residents. It involved three generations of the same family. It may also have a basement. The owners are trying to locate it and the entrance to the tunnel. At one time there was a slaughterhouse on the back of the property. Last year it was brought up that there may even be a cemetery on the property. This would explain the odd steps going to the lot on the side of the house. Someone who knows how to find lost graves claimed to have been able to determine there were slight indentations in the ground on the side yard that may be graves. It also explains some of the stones placed in one corner on that side yard. To date it hasn't been investigated but it is in the future. There are so many things to explore when it comes to HHH. Some think there may be a body that's more recent buried somewhere on the property. A number of people have said it is there. This relates to a murder where someone has confessed but failed to disclose where he put the body. The missing female did know people at this house during the time she went missing. There is also an unsolved murder where the body was missing about a year. She was last seen in front of this house and knew people who lived there at that time. Her murder is still an open unsolved case. Items belonging to her and to the other female have been located on the property and identified by individuals who knew the women. The other murders are much older.

The Estes' own an empty lot next to the house. There had been a house there for many years. The city not only tore it down but removed the soil under the house and on the property, including the pipes for water and sewer. According to people living in town and in law enforcement the house ended up being a drug house run by a drug cartel. Allegedly there have been at least eight murders associated with that house. This lot has yet to be seriously investigated for paranormal activity. But unexplained things have happened on the lot a few times.

This house has been rated by a number of sites as the #1 most haunted location in Texas and #1- #3 in the nation. Over 200 scratches have been documents in this house to date. Spirits seem to talk a lot and will join in on conversations that are recorded by security cameras. Not only do they join in on conversations, but they also talk about the future and may talk to specific individuals about personal information. There 18 rooms to investigate. The house was featured on Portals to Hell in 2020 and has been on other shows the past few years. Jack Osbourne told Rolling Stone magazine it is the scariest place he has ever visited. He even said this to Ozzy and Sharon Osbourne during another Portals to Hell TV show. Clips of activity have been seen on Fright Night. Paranormal Declassified filmed an episode there as did Nick Groff for his show Death Walker. Those shows can be found on Discovery Plus. There have been interesting discussions about the house that were brought up in the Paranormal Declassified episode. Other shows are scheduled to film there in the future.

Anyone can rent entire property and stay all night. Check the calendar for open dates. They provide a wide variety of paranormal equipment for individuals to use, can provide history, videos and even an investigator to stay with the visitors. The Estes' do want everyone to understand due to the nature of activity this is an advanced site with several types of entities both negative and positive. Children are not allowed in the house. They have items from all over the world that are in the house. There are antiques, artifacts and a lot of dolls. Many of those are haunted. People come for birthdays, family reunions and just to hang out. These are not the paranormal investigators.

Many paranormal investigators and teams leave in the middle of the night scared. Now the Estes' stay overnight in a camper behind the house. Otherwise, they would show up the next day to a wide open house with all the lights on. Teams will sleep all together in one room, they have slept in their cars, under the table in the kitchen and even on the front porch. This is due to the high amount of activity they encounter. Many simply leave.

Phil owned the house until it frightened him so, much he refused to step onto the property. According to the Estes', Phil also had a camper behind the house he would stay. Even then he didn't like going into the house. The night that sealed the deal to not   go onto the property was the night he probably thought he might die. Phil was in his camper when suddenly there was a loud thud on the side of the camper. BAM! BAM! It happened a number of times. Then the camper began to shake and started to tip over with Phil inside. I can't imagine how I would feel if that were to happen when I'm in the camper in the back of the house. When the shaking and thuds finally stopped Phil looked outside. No one was there, nor had anyone been there while this occurred except for Phil. From then on, Phil met investigators on the street at the end of the driveway to give them the key to the house. The Estes said Phil's health began to decline while he owned the house. Now he has nightmares about the house, his health while improved is not what it used to be before owning the house. He isn't supposed to return to the house or even talk about it as his wife put her foot down about the house. Here is the account as told by Phil and given to the Estes' after they bought the house.

There were a number of paranormal teams investigating the house while Phil was the owner. I remember receiving several emails from Phil advising me I could come and investigate. Unfortunately, I was not able to make it to Mineral Wells before he sold the house. There were a few teams I know that did make it to the house. When the Estes bought the house, Phil gave them a large white notebook filled with information and research about the house. This is where I took some of the information, details and photographs to place in this book. Since buying the house, the Estes' have found out more about the house. Some of the history is not more accurate than what Phil comments on in his paper on the house.

Phil included investigation reports he received from Dallas Paranormal Alliance and Heaven & Hell Paranormal Investigators. Below is Phil's thoughts on the house and then I will highlight the two investigations.

The history as told by Phil Kirckhoff...........

History of Hill House

I first saw Hill House in February of 2013. Upon first seeing the house I immediately fell in love with it and the surrounding property. My main goal then became to buy the house and surrounding property. My plan was to take the next 7 years, restore it and then retire to a paid off house. I was able to finalize the purchase of the property in June of 2013. Little did I know at the time how haunted Hill House was, how it would change my plans and life.

Built in 1898 little is known of the house or its' history. Oddly enough it seems as though the house has come in under the radar for 115 years. I have looked in three books and over 1,000 photos from the late 1800's on and there are no pictures of the house. I have done extensive research on the internet, reviewing books and interviewing old time Mineral Wells residents. There are no written stories of the house or its history as of this writing. Further no one really remembers it.

The house is extremely haunted with much activity. The amount and type of activity has caused me to have to cancel my plans of living in the house. The former owners contacted me recently and related many of their own stories of paranormal experiences they had while living in the house. They said for years they lived with the house ghosts and just accepted them. Then about two years ago something came to the house that caused them so much trouble they simply left the house in the middle of the night never to return until they met with me. They experienced bed sheets being pulled off at night, seeing apparitions. One person was held and choked. They would hear a voice talking to their baby at night on the baby monitors. The claim was one night upon hearing the voice talking to the child saying, "you are ours and we will keep you", that was when they left.

The neighbors and former residents claim the house to be haunted by multiple spirits. They claim many spirits inhabit the house but the three that are most prominent and have been experienced since the purchase is: a little boy, a woman in a blue dress and a shadowman.

The old lady in the blue dress is called the guardian and seems to protect the house and appears to children very readily. The little boy has two stories one the house was a bordello in the late 20's early thirties. One of the working girls had a child that was deformed and mongoloid. He lived one of the small upstairs rooms until he passed away at about 6 years old. He is very curious and will interact with you after you have been in the house for an hour or so. I have been told he will throw balls back downstairs if you toss them up. All but red ones and he keeps those. Former residents claim he likes noisy push toys and will play with them in the night. Sometimes they had to put them up so they could sleep. The Shadowman has caused issues and has been reported to follow people home, causing sleep paralysis in two instances and throwing things in one.

Neighbors and past residence also claim the house is a portal and twice a year you will see residual apparitions walking the house and property. Soldiers to ladies in frilly dresses all walk the property.

Current Verified Experiences

July 21st we were preparing for a group meeting at my house. I heard something stomping upstairs and kept asking my wife which one of our children had come home. She kept telling me no one was upstairs. She finally said that was the noise she had been hearing. Later that night my daughter came in and said who had been in her room as a glass had been broken and two of her cameras had been thrown across the room. When we told her of the noises she heard earlier she went to her friends to spend the night as she was too scared to sleep in her room. My older daughter said early the next morning she was going to get up to go to the bathroom and something was holding her arm so that she could not get up. The experience upset her to tears. Here are her own words of what happened:" It was like I woke up turned off my alarm went back and laid down, the second I did I felt something roll literally on top of me and started squeezing like my whole body and my throat. It freaked me out so I tried screaming but it was like my voice was being choked out so I tried pushing it off and it like grabbed my arm and tried pushing me back down. This like happened for I dunno two or so minutes and I finally pushed it off. When it was off I was both scared and angry and just felt this "hahahaha" feeling"

8/10 and 8/11. I spent a few hours each day in the house trying to clean it up. Two friends came by on Saturday and one said he saw a flash at the top of the stairs. On Sunday I was there for a while moving furniture. A friend came over and helped and we discussed an Estate sale we would do the weekend after Labor Day. We both smelled cigar smoke very strong in the front foyer. My friend saw an AXE head with the handle broken off in the floor. There is a ring of what looks like dried blood around the axe head. The axe head was not there on Saturday; my friends from Saturday said it was not there. I moved furniture Sunday morning prior to my friend coming over. I cannot prove it but the axe handle was not there. I have pictures of the axe and the blood stain.

8/13/2013 I spoke with my friend that was at the house with me Sunday He said Monday night something came into his room and he had a fight with it he said it felt like it was crushing him. He said he had a spiritual battle with it and it left. He said he felt when it left.

8/17/2013 My Mom and Dad came to the house to check it out. I had been mowing the lawn and they knew I would be there. My Mom took two paintings left in the house by the previous owners. The next weekend she was hanging them up. She said when she hung the last picture she felt dizzy, nauseous and a crushing feeling on her chest. She had to go to the hospital. She was released the next day with nothing showing on the tests. I mention this as the other two that had been visited felt crushing feelings on their chests.

8/27/2013 My older daughter Mollie (she was visited by the spirit at home see July 21st) and I went to the house about 10:00PM. There was a production company filming a Zombie movie up and down the street my house is on. I had never been to the house at night and it was an experience. I felt I was being watched the entire time. When we left we were sitting in front of the house in my Jeep. My daughter wanted to take a picture she took one through the front class of the Jeep. I told her to get a better picture to take it out the window. I turned the jeep so she could. The picture has a definite mist in it not unlike many pictures I have taken during the day.

Sunday September 8, 2013, I was the first one in the house. The kitchen door was wide open. We have never opened it and it has a latch that can only be opened from the inside. I was the last one out and the door was not open.

Saturday September 7 2013 We had an estate sale at the house a large number of people showed up. Many that went upstairs said they felt the woman some said they could feel the little boy. One visitor said there was something about the steps that would be good for me. She could not say what she was pointing towards the 5th step on the stairs. I did not know what that meant at the time but do now. That will reveal its self later in the stories. But a great deal of the activity is centered around the 5th step on the stairs. Later that day about 3:00PM the huge crowd of people that kept coming in to buy items at the estate sale had calmed down.

Saturday Sept 7, 2013- I had my strongest paranormal experience ever. My friend Doug Sheppard and I were standing at the foot of the stairs. My friend said "Wow i just felt a charge hit my chest." I said i was feeling the same. He then said it is going around my arms. I said the same thing is happening to me. I had the hair on my arms standing up. I then said to him it has traveled down to my legs. He admitted the same. There was a definite swirling around my legs. I then felt it move to my head. Doug said he was feeling the same. This went on for about two minutes. The sensation was that of very cold air and static electricity at the same time. The feeling was not bad at all as if it was checking us out. My friend pulled out his cell phone to text the experience to his girl friend. He showed me his cell phone and in the text box was the word Memphis. Later a neighbor stopped by to introduce himself. He went upstairs, came rushing back down said, "this house needs to be in a movie". I asked why and he stated it is just too haunted,. When I questioned him further he said a rush of super hot charged air hit his chest. He left very quickly mumbling this is a haunted house for sure.

Friday September 13 My daughter was talking to me with her hand on the stair case. Said her hand felt like someone was touching her. This went on for approx. 60 seconds until she had to move her hand

Saturday Sept 14 Having an Estate sale large numbers of people coming out:

1. Multiple people indicating they felt something
2. One lady said her cell phone in her back pocket was vibrating then realized it was her cigarette case that something was causing the sensation.
3. Three couples at different times went upstairs and while coming down at the same spot said a left knee went out.
4. Four people said they had cell phone issues. One got a text supposedly from me telling them to come back. One got a text unknown from an unknown sender. Her phone then went out. It was so trashed ATT has to send it back to the factory.

PREVIOUS OWNERS OF HAUNTED HILL HOUSE

W hile the house was built earlier than was Sonny and Katherine thought the information and names of owners I have only goes back as far as 1884. But the house was built 10-20 years earlier. Here is the information the Estes' received from previous owner Phil Kirckhoff when they purchased the house.

1884 – Fannie Yeager

1890 - CF Yeager, looks like it may include an additional lot

1907 – John Renfro (I have located a second spelling for this name, Rentfro and not sure which is correct)

1939 – John Renfro to E.O. Chapman

1941 – E.O. Chapman to B. Chapman and then somewhere over the next few years it was back to E.O. Chapman

1944 – There are two different owners selling to two different people – U.S.W. Williams to W.G Chapman and then B.E. Chapman to C.D. Chapman

1945/1946 – U.S.W. Williams W.G. Chapman

1946 – E.O. Chapman to D.D. Brian

1948 – Shows three transactions of ownership, D.D. Brian to W.A> Davidson, then W.A. Davidson to C Welch and finally W.A> Davidson to L.J. Kincanon

1952 - D.D. Brian to State National Bank

1955 – Grace Cox to L.J. Kincanon

1957 – L.J. Kincanon to Carrie Kincanon whom transferred property to J.P. Williams

1970 – Once again the property went through three owners, M.W. Building & Loan to L.J. Kincanon whom sold to John Johnson who then sold to F.C. Meyers

1975 – John Johnson got the property back and sold to Charles

Greengard who then sold it to Duncan Graut (sic)

1985 – The estate of Doris Greengard had the property and sold to Gary Morris who then sold to Orville Grantham

1986 – Orville Grantham sold to Charles Greengard

1990 – Greengard sold to Don Tabner who sold to John Moore

1991 – Another owner, Marvin Wittman sold to F.C. Meyers

1994 – Ownership was back to Marvin Whittman who sold it to Trinidad Caston. Records also show another owner as Don Tabner who sold to Melissa Kavacavich who then sold to George Graut (sic)

1997 – Melissa Kavacavich to David Kavacavich and there were other owners recorded in the same year as Charles E. Greengard to Don Tabner who sold it back to Melissa Kavacavich who sold it to Trinidad Caston who sold it back to Melissa Kavacavich.

1997- More exchanges of ownership occurred as Melissa Kavacavich sold it to Delbert Montgomery who sold it to Michael Hard who then sold it back to Delbert Montgomery

1998 – Delbert Montgomery sold it to Mark Clingings

2009 The property went from Mark Clingings to Molly Clingings in a divorce. She is related to Delbert Montgomery.

2010 – Palo Pinto General Hospital released a lien on the property back to Molly Clingings

From there the property was under control of Federal Home & Loan for an unknown period of time. It then went to Dyck & ____ (name unreadable). Then it went to another individual who eventually sold to Phil Kirckhoff.

2018 – Phil Kirckhoff sold to the current owners, Katherine and Sonny Estes.

This was just as confusing to put down in a timeline as it may have been to read. The notes I had were handwritten by another person. Some of the last names may have been misspelled but I did my best. It's interesting how many times the house has transferred back and forth at times to the same people. From the time Delbert Montgomery and Molly Clingings, father and daughter, had the property it appears they were family that stayed the longest.

The Estes' own the lot next door and I have not seen any ownership records for the property. It is usually to house shown across from the Baker Hotel and next to the church. For some reason Haunted Hill House is rarely seen in old photos. Some photographs of town do show the water tower on East Mountain behind the other house. The Estes' own the property behind both lots almost all the way up the mountain.

The welcome sign was once behind the house and is said that it was the sign that inspired the Hollywood sign. Footings for the water tower and sign have been located by the owners. It seems like the more they look for answers and historical documentation of people and events, the more there is that's located.

Date	From	To	Type	Amount
	5-10-18	Edward & Katherine Estes		
		Kirckhoff	Cont 20 50/07	
	Eyck	Yi	Cond 2013/1	
	Fed Home Loan	to Eyck & Kidline	ASM 2005-8	
7-08-2010	Palo Pinto General Hospital	to Molly Clingings	Hospital Lien	1681.8
15-2010	Palo Pinto General Hospital	to Molly Clingings	Hospital Lien	1181.2
1-23-2009	Mack Clingings / Molly Clingings	Divorce	# 42,085	
1-21-1998	Delbert Montgomery	to Mark Clingings	Contract	978.74
13-1997	Delbert Montgomery	to Michael Hood	DT	910.718
13-1997	Melissa Kovacevich	to Delbert Montgomery	WD	910.715
13-1997	Trinidad Castan	to Melissa Kovacevich	WD	910.710
13-1997	Don Tabner	to Melissa kovacevich	Rel	(826-710) 910.708
13-1997	Charles E. Greengard	to Don Tabner	Rel	(514.81) 910.706
13-1997	Melissa Kovacevich / David Kovacevich	Divorce	# 35,794	
23-1994	Melissa Kovacevich	to George Gault	DT	826.714
23-1994	Don Tabner	to Melissa Kovacevich	WD	804.70
23-1994	Marvin Wittman	to Trinidad Castan	WD	813.761
22-1991	Marvin Wittman	to F.C. Meyers	DT	215.931
21-1990	Charles Greengard	to Don Tabner	WD	746.503
21-1990	Don Tabner	to John Moore	DT	216.81
6-1986	Orville Grantham	to Charles Greengard	Trustee Dead	(184.465) 662.353
29-1985	Gary Morris	to Orville Grantham	DT	184.465
29-1985	Est of Doris Greengard	to Gary Morris	WD	655.743
	Estate of Doris Greengard	# 5893		
24-1975	Charles Greengard	to Duncan Gault	DT	120.172
24-1975	John Johnson	to Charles Greengard	WD	464.97
10-1970	John Johnson	to F.C. Meyers	DT	98.105
10-1970	L.J. Kincanon	to John Johnson	WD	374.720
25-1970	M.W. Building & Loan	to L.J. Kincanon	Rel	374.82
1-1957	L.J. Kincanon	to J.P. Williams	DT	65.82

2-19-1957	L.J. Kincanon / Carrie Kincannon	Divorce		262.36
8-17-1955	Grace Cox	to L.J. Kincanon	Rel	252.264
1-25-1952	D.D. Brian	to State Natl Bank	Transfer	233.606
1-20-1948	W.A. Davidson	to L.J. Kincanon	WD	215.151
3-22-1948	D.D. Brian	to W.A. Davidson	WD	214.452
3-05-1948	W.A. Davidson	to Cora Welch	DT	47.183
1-20-1946	J.S.W. Williams	to W.G. Chapman	Rel	208.208
1-12-1945	J.S.W. Williams	to W.G. Chapman	Rel	201.385
3-13-1944	B.E. Chapman	to E.D. Chapman	ML	8.225
1-12-1944	J.S.W. Williams	to W.G. Chapman	Rel	144.296
6-19-1944	E.D. Chapman	to D.D. Brian	WD	208.208
1-10-1941	E.D. Chapman	to B. Chapman	ML	7.628
1-23-1939	John Renfro	to E.D. Chapman	WD	186.413

1902 —

1890 — Lot 13 SF49-4

C.F. Yeager — SF4A Sc

1884

142496

They conducted their investigation October 31, 2013. They used a variety of equipment and trigger devices. The team set up, investigated some and left with Phil for a while. When the team returned, they discovered two trigger objects showed something tampered with them when no one was in the house. They left playing cards in a room and were in a different arrangement upon return. They left candy in one of the bedrooms and it had been moved. Some of their photographs showed possible light anomalies and a shadow of something. Their video evidence captured footsteps from upstairs, a loud bump noise and a male voice saying, "Yes." The team conducted an EVP session and had an EMF detector that was reacting to questions. There is possible evidence of something pushing a ball upstairs which occurred several times.

 Here is a list of some of the EVPS captured during the night while the team slept:

"Yes"

Bump sound from attic

Crying coming from upstairs

Whistling and mumbling

Moan

"Want to go home"

The handles on several suitcases were moved several times

Whispers

"Who is this?"

Furniture being moved

Sounds of a child running

A bang or bump that sounded like something hitting the pipes in the house.

The team spent 16 hours in the house during their investigation. They mention that not only the house, but a majority of Mineral Wells is built over a heavy concentration of rock and quartz in addition to all the mineral springs. Many in the metaphysical field believe quartz holds energy, conducts energy and the same with water. They think there is residual energy in the home. The team believed that the house itself is holding onto the energy of past inhabitants, good and bad. The team concluded HHH is haunted.

T his team conducted their investigation February 8/9, 2014, from 3:00 PM till 3:00 AM. That is when they left the house. The team collected a number of EVPS in the house and had a variety of personal experiences. They experienced residual and intelligent paranormal activity and believe the house to be haunted. Phil bought the house in 2013 and had plans to remodel the house and move into it with his family. It was when he began to remodel that activity began to pick up in the house. This is when he began to allow paranormal investigators to come to the house. This team went into the house to investigate with no information of the activity. Some teams choose to go into an investigation this way to see what they can glean from their evidence and personal experiences. Phil gave them a list of past owners in a sealed envelope after their investigation. Through EVPS the team got the names of a few past owners which they later confirmed from the list they got from Phil. They located two hidden crawl spaces and a "dummy" wall upstairs. I remember someone else discovered the hidden crawl spaces upstairs in 2020 while investigating.

Below are some of the personal experiences had by some of the investigators;

1. Upon entering the home this investigator picked up on a little boy downstairs. He was described as sad, withdrawn and with some sort of mental disorder. Since then the Estes' have learned his name is Joshua. He followed them around as they toured the house. That is – until they got to the Bootleg Room. This investigator saw a "man" look at them only to disappear into the crawl space. He was tall. Thin, wearing worn out trousers with a yellow and white shirt tucked in at the waist, slicked back hair and a thin mustache. He was seen off and on during the night. When the investigator went downstairs they got the feeling of something under their feet,

like a room. The words shackled and kept came into their mind. These words were repeated over and over while walking the outside of the house. They saw a quick vision of someone in a white lab coat and "Sick experiments" came to mind. At the back of the property there was an image of a baby and of something catastrophic with the baby. There was a feeling of several bodies buried on the property. This is something that is still discussed today. They were able to determine through research that some of the walls upstairs are part of a dummy wall system and horseshoe magnets were built into the design. That will give off false reading in those locations. One can often find wall systems such as this in buildings that housed illegal gambling, prostitution and bootlegging.

2. This individual was drawn to the closet under the stairs and felt a small boy inside. They came up with the name Jeremiah. He appeared to be 8-10 years old. He wore short pants with a matching jacket with a Peter Pan collar and skinny black tie that was tied in a bow. One sensitive with the team thought he may have been starved. They felt a female had died on the stairs. A male presence was felt in the Bootleg Room. A woman was observed in one of the bedrooms. At this time Phil only had two bedrooms, now there are five. It sounds like they are referring to the Shadowman Room. They felt someone in the closet. I have felt negativity in that closet many times. There was an imagine of a woman in pain and it was felt that she was that way due to either childbirth and forced sex. They felt there was someone buried on the west side of the house. And saw a table with a big round metal ball on one end and an old humped over man in a doctor's coat. Something fleeting that had to do with infants. They picked up on underground springs and a tunnel. Others have done the same. The investigator also felt there could have been a well under the house in the kitchen area. Since then it has been discovered there is most likely and well under the house.

They picked up in the living room a 14-15 year old female may have hung herself. The name Lucy was received and Lucy claimed she hung herself because she was told to do it. In area, unsure where, they picked up that it may have been servant's quarters. They spoke to a female who claimed to be the housekeeper but felt like she wasn't telling the truth and she may have had something to do with watching the children. A black male appeared and said he was in love with one of the women who slept in that room. He claimed they were caught being together and both were beaten to death. Several other entities were observed during the night.

3. While conducting an EVP session upstairs, their EMF meters were active. An EVP of Reverend Lang was recorded when asked who was with them. Both this investigator and her daughter felt something upstairs. The investigator became very cold and her daughter because extremely sad and began to cry. This has happened to a group of us at the same time while in the kitchen. The investigator felt like something from the house may have followed her home. She could feel something toughing her arm and she had four nights of dreams about the house. People still often have dreams of the house. Some before they get there and some after they leave.

4. This investigator heard a woman screaming downstairs. They also were touched several times. Since the investigation they heard bangs during the night and items being dropped on the floor at their home.

5. This investigator thinks they may have been visited by Toby the night before and called it "The Trickster." They had vivid visions of the house before going to the house. They smelled odd and unpleasant odors at the house and felt like they were "kicked in the butt by a spirit." This was after a ghost box session. They were talking whom they thought was a friend of Jacob's called Toby in the Carousal Room. They had gotten the name Toby several times during their ghost box session. They were also touched several times.

6. Another investigator had no personal experiences but had a successful session using an EMF meter. They captured a number of EVPS.
7. While in one of the downstairs rooms they got the image of a woman with pinned back hair. She looked tired, worn down and sweating.

In their historical research regarding the Reverend Lang EVP, it was discovered there was a minister by that name in Mineral Wells. He initially came to Fort Wolters as an Army chaplain.in 1941. He received a Bronze Star during his years of service and retired as a colonel. This is the team which complied the list of past property owners for Phil.

HAUNTED HILL HOUSE TODAY

PHOTO BY MARTHA HAZZARD DECKER

KATHERINE ESTES' RECOUNT OF
HAUNTED HILL HOUSE

I t all started when I was 6 years old. I had a dream that my uncle had fallen down the stairs and died. I ran to my father crying and he said it was just a dream. The next morning, I found out my uncle had indeed fallen down the stairs and died. Throughout my teenage years, my special gifts became much enhanced. I would hear many voices and thought I was crazy. It was to the point I didn't want to live. My gifts came in handy sometimes though. Like when I would play cards with my brother, I would always know which card to ask for in the game of Go Fish. I remember as a teenager finding out about people who had been murdered and in car crashes. My friends and I would go to sites and try to catch ghosts on my Walkman. After meeting my husband, Edward "Sonny" Estes, we both had a mutual attraction to knowing more about the afterlife due to both of us losing our fathers. We frequently visited Jefferson Texas for the ghost walks. On one occasion while there, a paranormal team had showed us a picture of three child spirits inside a house. That investigator said "why don't you visit this house, it's close to where you live". The home he was speaking of was Haunted Hill House. That is what began our attraction to Haunted Hill House. I started having visions of Haunted Hill House as if the home itself was calling me. So, we contacted the owner, Phil Kirckhoff, because we had seen the home was for sale. He made arrangements to meet with us. Our first visit to Haunted Hill House was more than we could have ever imagined. As Phil was showing us the home, I watched a giant green orb with my own eyes follow Phil around the house. It positioned itself behind me on the stairs at one point. We decided to go upstairs and check it out. We got a very dark and gloomy feeling; I have never liked it upstairs. While coming down the stairs we caught an EVP on our cell phone repeating words my husband had spoken. Yes, at that moment we knew the house was very haunted. Our first glance at the property was mesmerizing with the "Welcome" mountain in the back, it gave us a sense of country life in the city. All of the history we were told about the property was amazing. We contacted Phil two days later and purchased the home.

Before we purchased the home, I went online to look at the pictures of the house. I saw a ghost of a little boy in the window and Phil told me his name was Joshua, I told Phil that the boy is named Jacob, he is eight years old and died of asphyxiation. I believe the green orb following me and Phil around the house was Jacob. Remember the photo we saw in Jefferson from the paranormal team had two boys and one girl. Their names were Maddie, Joshua and Jacob. I believe Jacob called us to the home. After purchasing the home, I located journals from previous investigations that Phil had done and located a file that contained information about a boy named Jacob, eight years of age, whom was found hanging from a tree, death due to asphyxiation. I went outside and found a tree stump with a cross on it. One of the locals visited us and showed me the stump and told me that an eight-year-old boy named Jacob was found hanging from the tree in 1940 and died of asphyxiation.

Two weeks after owning the home I had a vision of two Native American chiefs arguing, one chief chopped the other's head off. I saw the past; these were the original settlers. They were coming down the mountain looking for water and found one of the wells. The water was tainted and caused hysteria and hallucinations. I saw this whole tribe as they began slaughtetng each other, even the children. Their blood ran into the well water and became a curse upon the land. During a later conversation with Phil, he stated there is a history book describing this vision I had. I always believed in seeing orbs and hearing spirits speak, but I never believed that spirits threw items. I thought that was faked for Hollywood. One day sitting outside the house having a cigarette on the back porch a large wheelbarrow was lifted in the air and thrown three feet at me. This was during the time we were leveling the house foundation. I ran screaming and the workers came to my rescue. One of the gentlemen came to assist me after hearing my scream. While placing the wheelbarrow back on the porch we both heard a loud gunshot go off, as if it was targeting him. In my state of panic, I contacted my physic friend Maria Elaina Santos Kempf to tell her what had happened. She said, "You bought a haunted house. What did you expect?". I told her I thought I was going to see orbs like in Jefferson, Texas. I didn't know they were capable of throwing things. Maria told me there was a dark entity in the home and I needed to be cautious about it. She said the entity was from a living person and a crime they had committed there. The crew that was leveling the house foundation had a supervisor whom was a Pentecostal preacher and I heard him correcting the workers. As they were searching for hidden tunnels under the house due to the rumors around town. I heard him shouting, "There is no such thing as buried treasure, no secret tunnels, no such thing as ghosts and y'all need the Holy Ghost!" Then he told them, "Get back to work". Immediately following this, the entire crew came running to the back, door yelling, "The pastor's nose is pouring with blood". We brought the pastor into the home and his nose was bleeding very bad!" As we attempted to stop the bleeding, the pastor said to me he had never had a nosebleed in his life. He wasn't overheated, and he did not scratch his nose. He also said to me he never believed in ghosts before and when they were bringing him into the home to treat his nose, he saw a little girl ghost in the living room and heard rustling in the bushes and felt as if someone was watching him. That pastor now believes in ghosts.

One month after owning the home an empath showed up out of nowhere begging me to allow her to read the home. She too was drawn to the home. She offered to pay me money to allow her to do this, so I obliged. During her reading of the home, we were recording live on Facebook and caught the most amazing EVP of a child crying at the well, "Mommy help me". I believe that child was Jacob. There have been times in the home where I have been growled at, items thrown at me and a very uncomfortable feeling. I personally have never experienced or dealt with paranormal activity of this magnitude. Sometimes I wonder what I have gotten myself into. I feel as though I am the caretaker of the spirits that are trapped within these walls. Even when I am at my personal home, I have woken up not knowing where I was, and my surroundings were at the Hill House at a different time period. Many people who have lived at or visited the Hill House have had re-occurring dreams just like mine, waking up in the Hill House even some that live out of state. It's like the Eagle's song, you can check in any time you like, but you can never leave.

Edward "Sonny" Estes Recount of Haunted Hill House

When I was twelve years old my father passed away. About four months after that happened, I woke up and looked over at the bed beside me, I saw a full apparition of my father watching me sleep. That was my first experience of seeing a ghost. After that I really didn't have any experiences until I met my wife, Kathy. Within the first year of being together, we began having experiences in our home in Parker County, Texas. Things continued to happen within our home that triggered us to investigate our surroundings. We started going to Jefferson. Texas and many other locations. We have had experiences in all of the locations we have visited. In April 2018 we were going to buy a haunted location. We visited one in Jefferson, Texas we were interested in and while there we were told about Hill House from a paranormal team. We visited Hill House. Within 20 minutes we had visual and audio experiences which were the confirmation we needed. It was like the house was showing itself to us, telling us to buy it. When we met with Phil, he told us that we were the last people to show the house. If we didn't buy it, he was going to close it up and wait for the Baker Hotel to purchase it for a parking garage. Since purchasing the home, we have encountered many unusual experiences. Such as, hearing children sing at night, running up and down the stairs and a child running its hands down the spindles on the banister. There have been people who have been scratched, bit and growled at and touched. One of the craziest things that have personally happen to me was when one night Kathy and I went to sleep in the Axe Room, I had a child laughing in my ear. I opened my eyes and a bright light flashed in my face. I believed it happened because Kathy put holy water around the bed before we went to sleep. Shortly after that an entity mimicked me and pulled the sheet down on my feet. We started recording and caught something looking at us from the crack in the bathroom door. That entity was Toby, a negative one. I have been to many haunted locations and have never experienced as much paranormal activity as I have at the Hill House. I enjoy being able to continuously experience paranormal activity at Haunted Hill House and watching others experience the magic of the home.

I want to know about the spirits, their lives, how they died and why they are still here. Our next door neighbor told us the property is a giant pathway for spirits to travel. He was a Shaman and has since passed. Our security cameras are able to catch many EVPS and we are getting different names .and conversations daily. They have confirmed my neighbor's statements.

I enjoy listening to the EVPS. It's like watching Days of Our Lives, only they aren't alive. There is never a dull moment, and you never know what will happen next. I look forward to many more crazy years at Haunted Hill House.

I conducted a lengthy interview with someone whom grew up in the house before it was known as Haunted Hill House. The names have been changed at the request of this person. The interview was transcribed from the recorded interview. I have also deleted parts of the interview. It will be released in another book in this series when I write about all the murders and deaths. I have interviewed another individual who lived in the house for two weeks. He left because he couldn't take the activity occurring in the house. While I have his permission to use his name, I will refrain from doing so as to not identify the individual in this interview. His name will be released in another book in the series. For the sake of this interview, we will call the person Sally.

M – is for me, the interviewer

S – is for Sally

M- Was your last name _____ when you lived here?

S- No, it was ____ and then ____

M- Phil has this document and it's really hard to read. It lists the owners of the house. It looks like people were buying it and then selling it to themselves then buying it again from themselves. But it looks as though a lot of people have been through this house through the years.

S- It wasn't for sale when we got it.

M-So when y'all got it, how old were you?

S- 4 or 5

M- You were little. When you moved here, who moved in with you. I know you had a lot of friends move in through the years. How many years were y'all here?

S-I was 19.

M- 5-19 that was a long time. So when you first moved in, who all lived here?

S- My mom, my dad my sisters, my brother and me.

M- How many sisters?

S- Two

M-Ok was this your dad or stepdad?

S- Stepdad, but he adopted me though.

M- Did anyone sleep upstairs?

S- Nobody slept upstairs

M- Can you tell me what it was like to live in the house?.

S- In which sense.

M- As a small child, what was it like growing up in the house?

S- It was hell growing up in the house. For me.

M- Why?

S- Because I was the one who saw everything, heard everything. I was always told that I was crazy.

M- So what was it that you saw and heard?

S- I just described them as monsters mostly, besides the lady. She was kind of the protector. Jacob was my only friend.

M- Let's start with the monsters. Tell me about the monsters.

S- They just stared a lot and just stood there. I didn't like the lights to go out because I would lose track of them.

M- Were they here when you moved in? What did they look like?

S- Kind of like one of the sleep projects.

M- What do you mean by sleep project?

S- Like when the government first started making amphetamines and was testing it on people. It's the only thing I've found that looks like it.

M- So in your words, describe it to me.

S- Demonic almost.

M- Are they 2 ft tall, 10 ft tall? 6 ft wide?

S- They're people, they are all different. They're usually skinny.

M- Tall, short fat? You said they're skinny so they're not fat.

S- Yeah they're like people.

M- Yeah but like what kind of people?

S- All different kind of people, that's the thing.

M- Yeah but what I'm asking is for your description as what they look like.

S- Demonic almost

M- Demonic, demonic looks, is different to different people.

S- I can't describe them.

M- Size wise, what size wise?

S- Very different sizes, tall and short.

M- How many different ones did you see?

S- I see a lot, I still see them, there's tons. I was diagnosed with schizophrenia effective disorder; my mom says that she doesn't think that I actually have it. It's the house that messed me up. But they still haven't gone away.

M- When you say tons that could be…

S- They're everywhere constantly

M- That could be 5 that could be 100

S- Thousands, I still don't like to turn off the light at night.

M- Sharp kind of pointy razor teeth

S- I woke up out of a dead sleep with them. At the time I was diagnosed, I drew that one. I was having night terrors; I've always had night terrors.

M- Everything from short to tall, all different sizes.

S- My mother was diagnosed with schizophrenia when we were living here. Then I was diagnosed as well.

M- I was almost convinced at one point that my mom was trying to kill me. You know because she's Wiccan. What do witches always do with their first born? And what do you do with ____?

M- Wiccan is really whitelighter. You have the two different; you have the dark and the light. The same as Voodoo. You have the dark and the light.

S- She always had her Voodoo dolls lying around here.

M- So she was more into the dark side of it.

S-I don't know. Me and my mom didn't mesh very well.

M- So you think she tried to kill you. What makes you say you think she tried to kill you.

S- I think that she wanted to kill me.

M- What makes you think that?

S- I came up with this theory. Like what does a witch do with her first born? They usually sacrifice them. What do you do with ____? You burn it. She almost treated me different than my sisters too.

M- How so?

S- Because they were silver spoon children. I was the redheaded step child locked in the shed.

M- Why do you think that was?

S- I don't know

M- Do you think because you were…..

S- I was different

M- How so were you different from them?

S- Probably because I was seeing things,.

M- Because you could see stuff.

S- I was more like my mom than them.

M- So your mom saw stuff

S-Um hum

M- What kind of stuff did you see?

S- Like my monsters, they were my friends, they were scary. After so long you get used to things like that. As a kid you see something in the corner of your eye walking around. Then bam they're right there. Yeah it's kind of scary. I do know that before the medication and everything though. I didn't know what eyeballs were. That was pretty cool to see all that.

M- You didn't know what eyeballs were?

S- Yeah, I knew how to draw and everything but I used to just put a dot. And then after they put me on the medications then I actually saw, it got brighter.

M- Because I know you knew what eyeballs were at 14.

S- Not really

M- I mean you knew you had eyes so…

S- I knew there was eyes but I don't know how to describe that. There's usually there usually that's how it started

M- Are you saying in your monsters, that they were just like spots or something Then their eyes became more like our eyes

S- There was just a glisten off of something but usually was darkness.

M- For the eyes

S- Well with everybody. People

M- For people, people too you didn't see they eyes. You just saw...

S- I would just see a skull drawing, a drawing like that.

M- Like that. That's what you saw. Even for living people?

S- Yeah.

M- That's pretty weird

S- That's how my middle son sees people too.

M- Really

S- When he first started showing signs. I noticed it right off the bat. I was saying that he was seeing things like I do. My husband was freaking out. "Why is he acting like this so much? Why can't I turn off the light. And don't turn off his lights." I still see them with the light on. It's not like he's afraid of the dark, he's afraid of losing track.

M- Kind of like Dr. Who…. Don't Blink

S- With the stone angels. I associate a lot of things with movies.

M- Are you visual, like when someone tells you something, you see it like a movie? What kind of things that were happening in the house while you were here.

S- There was one day. Whenever I was in the bathtub, I was thinking about Freddie Kruger, trying not to freak myself out. In the middle bathroom there was no windows, and the power shut off and I got stuck in the bathroom. The doorknob came off, the full nine yards. It was bad, I freaked out really bad on that one.

But, the door knob had never gone loose. It seemed like every time I got stuck in a room, the doorknob came off. It happened to me a lot. I even start thinking about anything you were afraid of. The power would start surging or just go off.

M- So what about ____?

S- Oh my brother was scared of everything, but he never really saw anything. He could feel it. He's my stepbrother though.

M- And your sisters?

S- They never really talked about anything. They said they don't remember. Whenever I did try to talk to them about thing happening in the house. I don't know if they blocked it out or they just don't want to talk about it.

M-That's possible.

S- Their friends didn't even know they had an older sister. I kind of disappeared. I was one of the missing persons after a while.

M- So what about your mom? What kind of things to your mom and dad?

S- I thought for a while that my mom or my dad was possessed. He would just randomly out of know where just blow up. The same thing with my mom though. With my mom it was mostly based at me. She'd blow up out of nowhere and throw things.

M- Not the monsters but the spirits, what was here when you moved here.

S- There's a few of the monsters, but there is the lady with the powder blue dress and Jacob. There's a guy that came through. He was really tall.

M- What kind of guy?

S- Army

M- Did you say Army?

S- Umhum

M- Was he in an Army uniform?

S-He always came from down the hill and goes through the door.

M- Down the hill

S- It happened every year around the same time.

M- So was it residual. If it was the same time every year, what time of year did it happen?

S- Fall, closer to November or October

M-But you would only see him that one time every year. I guess he was coming home from war or something.

S- I've read that there used to be a whorehouse at some point.

M- That's what they've been told. What else do you know about the house?

S- Like my experiences or what I've read?

M- No your experiences, your family's experiences. Not what you've read. Because I want to talk to you about your stuff.

S- It was just hell form me. I don't really want to discuss any of it. I came up here the last time about three years ago and they got to see everything go all nuts in the house. I can call them there. If you really want too, I can call them, just sit down.

M- They have lots of activity all the time.

S- They were saying at that point they hadn't seen the shadow man.

M- Three years ago. Do you have any idea who the Shadowman might be?

S-No

M- How do you describe the Shadowman?

S- He's a shapeshifter, stalker, changes.

M- Was he here when you moved or did he show up?

S- He was here. He was just watching at first. Then my sister brought in a Ouija board at some point here. I'm pretty sure she didn't close it out.

M- Did you use the Ouija board?

S- No, I refused

M- Who used the Ouija board? Both of them or just one of them?

S- Just one of them that I know of. ____ and her friends. I can feel energy off of it as I get closer.

M- Did they use it often?

S I have no idea, I wasn't here at that time. My mom just told me about it. I came back with my oldest son, while he was still a baby, and I didn't want to be there as soon as I walked it.

M- So while they were all here, you left, came back, left.

S- My mom would kick me out, then call the police and tell them I was a runaway.

M- Was one of your boyfriends living here too?

S- My middle one's biological father did at one point. Then my husband did at one point. Yeah, I had a boyfriend that lived here.

M-And then you said your husband?

S- Joe

M- Joe?

S- He was just let out of a psych ward not too long ago.

M- Does he have mental issues?

S- He lit himself on fire. He was fine at first. Whenever I contacted him the last time. Telling him I've been having dreams about the house again. It was whenever he started to flip, and everything went all crazy.

M-What do you think might have caused that?

S-It was calling out, and it does it every so often.

M- What is it?

S- I started having dreams of the house. I started having dreams as a kid in the house.

M- So What is it?

S- The house. Something is out of the house. I don't know what it is. Something stronger than what everybody talks about. I don't know. It's like it has a mind of its own almost.

M-So do you think it's something attached to the house or to the land?

S- Do you believe in past lives?

M- Possibly

S- I think it's something that happened in past life that no one has been able to dig up yet.

M- Past life of who?

S- My family

M-Your family?

S-Otherwise I wouldn't be here stuck here.

M- What kind of dreams do you have about the house?

S- The main one I have is seeing a small door in the wall of this room over here. And then going through it, it's a giant room and there's a girl in a glass case.

M- Small door in which room?

S= There's an add-on. That was my room.

M- The Shadowman room, it's what they call it?

S- No, that's to this side. The first room. Whenever you walk into the living room from back there.

M- The one they call the Scratch room now. The one that's got.

S- I don't know.

M- (Discussion about the rooms and drawing of the rooms in the house.)

S-My room was here.

M- So you're talking about what they call the Shadowman room. So your room was the Shadowman room.

M- Your Mom was in the front room on the other side of the kitchen, right?

S- My mom and Dad, wait, which one?

M- The room, if you're facing the front door on the left. Opposite of the stairs.

S- No, that was my sisters' room.

M- That was your sister's room? Which sister?

S- Both of them,

M-So your mom was in the other room with the fireplace and the bathroom.

S- They actually cut the whole in the wall to make a door for the bathroom.

M- Which room was your brother's room?

S- The one with the wood in…

M- That's the one they call the scratch room. These are the names that Phil gave them. They just kept the same names. Do you know what's behind the wall in that room? Because it should be the same length as the living room but it's not. Did you ever play in tunnels and other hidden places downstairs?

S- Yes

M- So where were those?

S- In the closet where we saw them at anyways. I don't know if there are any upstairs.

M- When you would get to the tunnels, this was in the walls downstairs.

S- Upstairs

M- Were there tunnels downstairs too or just upstairs?

S- There was just the one that seemed like a tunnel. It just went on forever.

M- Downstairs?

S- From the closet.

M- From the closet downstairs? Which closet?

S- The one in the living room; underneath the stairs.

M-When you would wake up upstairs, where would you be?

S- The dark room, right by the stairs. Did y'all find any cameras in there? My camera went missing whenever I was a kid. I've been looking for it forever.

M-Was it a 35mm?

S- I don't remember. My dad got it for me when I was got out of freshman year.

M- Did you put film in it?

S- No

M- You didn't have to put film in it.

S- No

M- Where was the last place you saw it?

S- In that in that room. When I was 14 in my room. I searched for years for it in that room. I just always assumed it ended up upstairs.

M- Why would you think it would have ended up upstairs?

S- That's where I always ended up. I'd go to sleep and ended up there all the time.

M- That's why I was trying to figure out what room you woke up in.

S- If you are walking up the stairs it was the one to the left.

M- The one to the left, Joshua's room.

S- Which one?

M- The one when you are going upstairs, the one to the left. Now they call that Joshua's room. Because Phil told them that's where Joshua had to stay in the house. What are your thoughts on that?

S- I don't think so.

M- Where do you think that Joshua stayed?

S- In what we had as a playroom. We never played up there. That's where I would always play with him.

M- Which room was the playroom?

S- The other one to the right. It has a little cubby hole you can crawl in. We I did.

M- The one to the right kinda behind the stairs sorta when you're walking up?

S- When you're walking up it's to the right.

M- So you've got a closet and then a room.

S- Yeah, the actual room.

M- So that room

S- The place where you would be scared to put your kid at because the window's too low. Yeah.

M- They are all low up there. So that's the room you think he stayed in. What makes you think that?

S- Behind the wall.

M- Behind the wall?

S- I thought that he was put behind the wall.

M- Did you pick up anything that was funny about Joshua or anything?

S- He had birth defects but. My mom called him a mongoloid. He didn't like that.

M- What kind of birth defects?

S- His face was caved in on one side. Kind of like Hunchback of Notre Dame.

M- Elizabeth was his mother?

S- I don't know

M- You don't know?

S- I think his mom was one of the whores.

M- So you mentioned a lady…

S-I think she was just one of the maids or something. She looked after the kids. She looked after all of us.

M- So you don't think she was Joshua's mother.

S- No

M- Do you know how he died?

S- I think just malnourishment from his mom locking him in that room. Trying to hide him.

M- What makes you think that?

S- I don't know. That's how I thought. I don't remember why

M- What about your brother's room, did you ever see anything in there?

S- His room is creepy. It scared me a little bit.

M- Why did it scare you?

S- Just the feel, even before you go in. It always seems like something was trying to pull you in to someone. It doesn't scare me like it did before.

M- Did anything happen to your baby when you lived here?

S- Whenever I was sitting with my mom, in my mom's room. Taking to her. I kept hearing whispering. I kept telling her to be quiet so I could hear. We'd hear a loud man's voice saying "I'm going to get you" At that moment that's when my son started screaming. And I left out. There's no way in hell. My daughter, who's never been in the house, she has the same dreams that I did as a kid. .

M- So did he ever get lifted up out of the crib or anything?

S- He was upstairs randomly. At the top of the stairs. Me and my mom would go check on him and he was upstairs. Which we had the stairs blocked off. He wasn't big enough to move anything. None of it was moved. He couldn't really climb or anything like that.

M- How old was he?

S- He wasn't even a year old yet. He was about 6 months.

M-He wasn't crawling or anything?

S- He was crawling and starting to walk. But no way could he have gotten to the top of the stairs.

M- So he didn't get lifted out of the crib, he just ended up upstairs?

S- He was in his crib whenever I left the room.

M- You found him upstairs?

S- Yes, there was one point when me and my mom walked in, he was just kind of…. You know. It looked like he was lifted.

M- He was in the crib. When you say he looked like he was lifted, what do you mean?

S- Like hovering almost. But I'm not positive on that one. I second guess myself a lot. I had to move furniture to get onto the stairs to get him. I don't know, that's the same spot that I was always playing with Joshua.

M- But you said that you didn't play upstairs.

S- Whenever I was real little, whenever we first moved in, we weren't allowed to play upstairs. My mom said I used to just sit up there. Talking to someone.

M- Do you know how come you couldn't go up there?

S- They said it was dangerous.

M- Do you know why?

S- There was a hole that fell into the fireplace behind my sister's wall.

M- That could be dangerous.

S- That and we were kind of rough. I think it's funny how I got contacted about the house right after I started seeing this other guy though.

M- Do you know who Toby is?

S- There's another kid.

M- Toby's not a kid.

S- I don't know about that, but there's another kid. She was quiet though.

M- Could that have been a Mattie? Because there's a story that there used to be apartments across the street from this house. She ran out in the road, got hit by a car and ended up dying on the sidewalk.

S- I don't know she was more like me. Kind of kept to herself and quiet.

M- So Toby is not good. You don't know the name Toby?

S- No

M- He makes a noise like a growl. Like a person, not an animal making a growling noise. What about the piano?

S- That was my piano, it makes noise. That's why it went from my room to the hallway. I can't sleep with it.

M- What about your brother's room?

S- I slept in there sometimes, but nothing messed with me in there.

M- Did other people get scratched?

S- My brother and my Stepdad, some of my brother's friends, our cousins.

M- (Talking about people who really are demonologists vs the fakes and the scratcher room) Do you know what is in that room?

S- Sleep projects

M- Some if those monsters?

S-Yes. Technically the sleep projects were not human. They were experiments.

M- You never heard of Toby. What about when you go up the stairs and you go straight into that room. Was that your playroom?

S- We didn't go in there much. We weren't really allowed in there much because you could fall in through the floor. We watched a dog fall through the floor.

M- They call that room the bootleg room because they found bottles from prohibition in the cubby holes.

S- We found them up on the hill.

M- And you hid them in the cubby holes?

S- We hid them everywhere. We found lots of stuff. We would go up the trails up the hill and find things. We found a gas mask up there too. Found a sword: that was pretty cool.

M- It's really grown now.

S- Me and my brother went up there with a machete.

M- Did you find anything else in the woods? It wasn't as much woods as now when you were here? How about where the travel trailer is now?

S- There was a barn here. They tore it down. There was a garage part on one side then there was the barn part that had a loft like fenced in stall for chickens.

M- Did you ever find any weird stuff close to here?

S-Old newspapers and bottles filled with we don't even know what.

M- What did it look like?

S- Like black sludge?.

M- Were they canning jars or bottles?

S- Some of them were but they sometimes had hard pieces. We would take them apart, open them up.

M- Did you ever find any bones or anything?

S- We found all sorts of bones. We swore we found fingers. Mom told us they wasn't but dad told us they was.

M- So you don't really know because you don't have those anymore. Where exactly were you finding that stuff?

S- We were digging around up in the loft. We weren't supposed be in there. I still think my dad would beat my ass if he found out.

M- So you found those in the loft. Was like an old barn that had been here a long time with the house? Those weren't in the woods or the ground where you were searching?

S- We found all sorts of jars out in the woods too.

M- But those you found in the barn loft. So when you found the jars were they in any particular area?

S- Explains the location of the barn. We had a garden we were growing out there.

M- What about that stone thing that's out there? It's been called a BBQ pit and an altar. Part of it's natural but part of it's not. It was something built.

S- Which one?

M-It's right out here and I pointed to it. A giant rock with other rocks kind of looks like a horseshoe shape.

S- Does it look like it could be caves underneath the big rock? We used to play in it and there was just an eerie feeling we couldn't see anything in there.

M- Some people say it was used was an altar. It was used as an alter for wiccan or occult type stuff.

S- Kind of what it looks like that. Yeah

M- So do you know anything like that?

S- I know that whenever we bought the house, it was devil worshippers that owned it. I don't know how my mom even got in contact with these people if she wasn't a part of it honestly. That's just my opinion. But I still think that my mom would've sacrificed me.

M- Let's see who had this before. Y'all did. Do you know what their last name was?

S- No

M- Who is ____?

S- My grandpa

M- Your grandpa? This is really confusing on this because of the times and dates and all. (It shows (you are explaining the deed timeline and all the different and reoccurring names.) You mentioned Michael Horne?

S- I don't know the guy. I guess that's the guy who was after us.

M- And then back to your grandfather and back to your stepfather

S- My grandfather, really?

M- He had it and then your mom had it. And then in 2010 is says....

S- Hmmm, can I write that down?

M- Sure, then it says that Palo Pinto General Hospital had the house, had a lien on the house for taxes.

S- Oh yeah, whenever my mom lost it, but she left in the middle of the night. She didn't tell anyone she moved out.

M- So your mom left in the middle of the night. Why did she do that?

S- Something got a hold of her husband she says. I don't know because I wasn't here.

M- What about Jacob, do you know anything about Jacob?

S- Yeah that was the first one that I was talking about.

M- Tell me about Jacob?

S- Just another one of those was kind of quiet but he was always smiling.

M- Yes, (You tell a story about reading an old book storybook to the children in the house)

S- I read to them. When I was pregnant, I would sing to them a lot. I kind of took the place of the woman who cared after us.

M- The woman who what?

S- Cared after us.

M- And you don't know what the woman's name was?

S- No she was the woman with the blue powdered dress. She like cared for us.

M- How did she do that?

S- Every time my mom would go after us. She would stand in front of her sometimes whenever we were really little. Kind of a guardian angel in a sense.

M- Do you think she was there for Joshua?

S- Yes, and Jacob.

M- How bout on the sealed up bathroom. Was that sealed up when y'all lived here?

S- Yeah, my dad pushed me through the window.

M- But you never unsealed it.

S-No, we just looked around.

M- Did your folks ever have any kind of wiccan stuff they did while you were here?

S- My mom

M- What kind of stuff did she do?

S- She did tarot cards, palm readings. It was more for fun for her. She had a few different little voodoo dolls. I had a bunch of weird stuff like she did. She locked herself in her room a lot.

M- Did you ever see her do any other kind of stuff, more of a dark magic or anything?

S- I don't really know, like I said she locked herself in her room a lot. Was talking weird stuff.

M- Did she have an altar?

S- There's one upstairs

M- Where upstairs?

S- In the playroom.

M- That's the one that's kind of behind the stairs on the right?

S- Yeah

M- What did the altar look like?

S- It was just wooden. There were random splotches of rust from what it looked like.

M- Random splashes of what?

S- Rust

M- OK, on the wood altar

S- Umhum

M- Which could or couldn't be, might or might not be blood? You can really speculate on that.

S- Yeah, that what she's gonna say.

M- Did your mother ever get choked here?

S- Yeah

M- Tell me about that.

S- I was in the other room, I was across the hallway in what was my sister's room when they were still here. I just heard her screaming. I didn't see her.

M- The house that was next to y'all. Was that a dope house?

S- They smoked a lot of pot..

M- Did your mom ever go to sleep and wake up in the wall?

S- Over by the fireplace.

M- Which fireplace?

S- Over in their room.

M-Do you remember how she got out of there?

S- She said she kept walking. Kind of like how I did whenever I woke up in the upstairs bedroom.

M- I think she had said that, according to Phil. That she woke up in the walls and followed a light and came out in the living room.

S- How would that go?. Probably out of the closet because we used to play in the closet all of the time.

M- The closet would go by the fireplace. That would make sense.

S- Yeah probably the closet. How it's like underneath the Baker, the tunnels.

M- Yes

S- With this being one of the first houses built in Mineral Wells. It wouldn't surprise me if there were tunnels to here too.. We always thought there were tunnels underneath the hill.

M- There may be because there's always talk of tunnels. Did you ever play in any?

S- Underneath the Baker. We made a friend with a homeless dude. I was always trying to make sandwiches and stuff for people that were out walking around daily that I would recognize.

M- So where do you think those tunnels are located on this property? How far were you able to follow them? Did you play in very far?

S- They didn't go very far. I was afraid of the dark and insects. I just didn't want to try it.

M- There was a pentagram on the floor in one of the rooms.

S- Which room?

M- I don't remember which room.

S- Upstairs?

M- Did y'all draw a pentagram somewhere?

S- We, me and my sisters… well I can't vouch for them. I didn't. I know my mom put some weird stuff on the flooring in my room. I don't know, I'm always trying to prove that my mom was trying to kill me. She was hurting me a lot. Every time I tried to tell the police or something, they would never do anything.

M- When you said hurt you. What do you mean by that?

S- My mom beat the **** out of me. Because I was born. I was the reason everything went wrong in her life. That's what she told me anyway.

M- Do you know about any kind of writing that's under the house?

S- We climbed under there and found bottles and old books

M- Did you find bones under there?

S- Yeah, we would climb all the way to the back. Play hide and seek.

M- Did you ever know if there some kind of writing on or under the house?

S- There's something there but we could never make it out and my mom was always taking our flashlights from us.

M- Was there something built under the house with rocks? Do you know something about that?

S- I didn't know what it was but yeah it's been there.

M- So that was there when y'all lived here?

S- My mom just told us to leave it alone.

M- So you never did figure out?

S- By the time I could just run off and her not paying any attention to it. I was too big to get underneath there and climb all the way back.

M- Did you ever see an opening into it or was it just totally sealed off?

S- It wasn't sealed off. You could move rocks and stuff around it but it was dirt.

M- Did you ever go into it? Or could you see into it?

S- Umum, it was always too dark under there.

M- Were there any deaths in the house while y'all lived here?

S- Any what?

M- Deaths, did anybody die while y'all were in the house?

S- Not that I know of. (mumbles something). I don't know, there were a bunch of people that were messed up over here. The party house going on. My dad, he would always hang out with us. My mom never would. She'd lock herself in her room.

M- Is there anything else you can think of?

S- No

M- My last question, I asked you if you know if anybody died in the house. What about Krishonda? (She went missing on July 5, 2010. She was last seen possibly at this house. There is a photograph taken that date of her at this house. She was missing for a year until some of her bones were discovered)

M- I know in the front of the house. Up by the front of the house, there's a big round white thing that has a bunch of junk right now. Do you know what the heck that was?

S- Where at?

M- It's up by the front of the house it's right against the house and the porch. It's like a big round you know cylinder, like a pipe. It's in the ground.

S- It's for a water spigot.

M- It's too big for a water spigot.

S- It had a water thing that came out from it.

M- That's weird.

S- It's just to keep it enclosed in case a pipe busted up top. We had a dog, a guard dog but he got out randomly. He chewed up everything,

M- That thing is really tall, it's up above the porch and it's big.

S- It used to collect water too.

M- Yeah I'd bet.

S- I think there might have been a well underneath it to collect.

M- What about the well that is in the back yard?

S- I never messed with it.

M- Did you ever get water out of it? Or was it already sealed up?

S- I think it was already sealed up. Not too sure. I know my dad made us kids tear down the barn. We used my boyfriend at the time's truck.

M- Is there anything else you can think of?

S- No, Mineral Wells keeps a lot of secrets.

M- That's what I keep hearing,

S- As small as this town is, it's full of secrets.

M- Are you saying I didn't get a lot or that I got more than most people?

S- I answered questions as they're asked.

M- Well that was a question.

S- I just answered your questions as they're asked. Everyone has a life, right?

M- Everyone has a what?

S- A life. You don't remember anything if you're out under pressure.

M- I didn't feel like I was really putting you under pressure.

S- I never said you were. On the spot would be a better used word. Just Through dreams.

M- Just through dreams, what does that mean?

S- Nightmares, night terrors I've had. Like the little girl in the case. It looked like she was alive.

M- Oh yeah, where was that?

S- My daughter's had the exact same dream. She explained it to me word for word. I never told her about it.

M- Would you tell me that again about that dream.

S- You go through a small door.

M- That's right, now where was the small door?

S- Next to my bed on the wall. The far wall.

M- By the closet?

S- Umhum

M- Ok

S- You go through and then you're in a big room. It's down

M- Down? What do you mean it's down?

S- To go into the big room because it's stone.

M- Oh stone. Did you walk downstairs?

S- I never went that far.

M- Ok, and you said what looked like a girl.

S- There was a girl I can draw her.

M- A girl in a glass case. What'd she look like?

S- Blonde hair, really pale skin. Her eyes were bright blue; bright, bright blue. I only saw her eyes open once though. So far my daughter hadn't seen her eyes open.

M- So was this a dream you've had more than once then?

S- Reoccurring

M- Somebody, if they can save their butt. They'll roll over on somebody even if they're making it up.

S- Yeah

The complete interview will be in the book I plan to write about the murders and deaths in this house. The early murders, there were at least six I'm aware of plus a few deaths which were more of a natural nature or an accident or two.

What is interesting are the words which came up in an app on my phone while I was editing the interview. I wasn't talking during the editing. I will add the words here and you can draw your own conclusion. But I would like to hear your thoughts on it.

Words displayed on a phone app called Ghost Hunting (but I don't actually "ghost hunt." I prefer to conduct an investigation or do research. While I enjoy the paranormal, it is not a form of entertainment to me, unless I'm at a friend's house or watching TV. I have often found the words and phrases that come up on this app to often apply to an interview or place I am at. For example, a friend and I were in a cemetery, and she had the app open. No one was talking. We were on our way out when she trips over a headstone partially buried in the ground. She looks at the app and the name on the headstone is on the app. I don't know…

It's interesting how some of them correspond to what I am writing at the same time. The words from beginning to end; conditions, cast, he knew, keep away, window, leaf, specter, three, indication, laughter, cost, trim, cold baby, airline, spot, high, confuse, genesis, cave, branch, spirits, cost, chance, harvest, sample, strength, sponsor, porch, size, arm, think, intensity, Debbie, passed, thick, facility, pierce, refrigerator, me, body, nice, warp, gentle, abort, entirely, satisfaction, remove, whole, enough, touched me, sky, insects, trouble, evil, soon, bicycle, Anna, speak, persist, Persian, Alexis, justify, pay, choose, chicken, quietly, Charlotte, jacket, Leo, saw, divide, John, rusts, coverage, crawl, vision, exclude, just, placebo, view, near, angry, tragic, equally, England, reflect, bring him, Cody, the noise, belly, rival, devil, dirt, sit, tremor, succeed, patch,

What I can say about my experience with the app is that in the few years I have had the app these are the most words it has ever spit out. If you go back through the interview, you may see how many of the words actually correlate with it. I was speaking with a friend about the book and how it was coming along a few days ago. She said she thought it was almost time to end it and save the rest for the upcoming books in the series. Maybe while editing the interview something else was trying to tell me the same. What do you think?

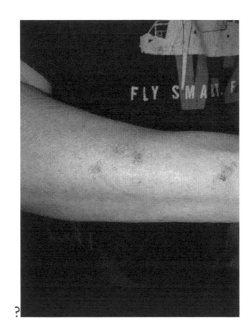

There have been so many experiences at this house I could go on forever. Just know there will be many more experiences to come.

Sheila Gay

My radio show "Rogue Talk Radio" did a live FB feed from Haunted Hill House August. There is a feeling of spirit everywhere in the house. My husband was hearing children's voices in the front hallway and when he went to check it out no one was there. We captured an EVP upstairs in the bootlegger's room of a child's voice saying help. My personal experience was one of the most unusual that I have had in over 10 years of investigating. I was doing a sensory deprivation session. I was blindfolded with earbuds plugged into a ghost box and noise cancellation headphones over the ear buds. I was laying in the bathtub where it is reported that a prostitute had committed suicide. One of the very first things that happened was I felt a sensation on my left arm like a pinch and burning, I rubbed my left arm with my right hand(as you can see in the live FB feed). The session continued with me saying all the words that were coming through the ghost box. I felt as if something was trying to pull my legs down, so I bent one leg to steady myself. It was truly the most unnerving feelings I've ever had during an investigation. I finally felt as if there were too many souls in that small bathroom with me. I was overwhelmed and had to stop the session. My adrenaline was pumping, my hands and voice were shaking for over 10 minutes. We continued the investigation until about 6:00 am. I didn't even notice the mark on my arm until the next day. When I sent the picture of the mark to Katherine the owner of Haunted Hill House, she told me several people had been bitten in that very room.

Sheila Gay (She was a wonderful full of life and fun loving friend)

Co-founder of Northeast Texas Paranormal Society

Host of Rogue Talk Radio

Co- founder of The R.I.F.T. Radio Network

Sheila and I were at many of the same paranormal conferences over about 10 years. This is how we met. We, and others would hang out, eat meals and have fun in the evenings talking about adventures and life in general. She passed in 2021 and will be missed by the many who loved her. Wherever she is, Sheila is probably doing what she did best, exploring her new world. Love you lots my friend.

Peter James Haviland A.C.C.H.

It was back in the early to mid 2000's when I first heard of Hill House. I had come out of The Baker Hotel, after doing some research for the then owners, when I started hearing the wild stories about this house on the hill behind the Baker. Some of the things I heard about were sounds of footsteps, voices and things that made the owner really scared to even live in the house. I also heard of folks leaving the house in the middle of the night due to being terrified. I had driven up the hill and talked to the folks that were renovating the home, they were replacing carpet and what looked like other flooring. They confirmed some of the stories I had heard and added that there was something on the second floor that made anyone staying up there leave in the night or they would leave almost right after going up there. He told me that IT didn't like people, but he wouldn't go into more detail. Well, the house piqued my interest over the years, and I sometimes wondered what other things were going on there, but Mineral Wells was a long drive and as you know, life takes us on the paths we travel.

I have known Martha for many years. We met through conventions where we both appeared and became good friends. We have many things in common, private investigation being one. I truly respect her as she has always been there for me, and we always discuss cases and ideas with each other. Martha started telling me about Haunted Hill House one night and said she had met Kathy and was looking into the house. Well, that was exciting, as I always wanted to see what was going on there and Martha mentioned to me that she would get Kathy Estes and I to meet.

Martha came up to me at a convention we were both attending and introduced me to Kathy Estes, the current owner of the house and we hit it off right away. I told her how I visited the house many years ago and what I knew about the home. I remember sitting up with her and Martha late one night while Kathy shared with us what was currently going on out there, she even shared some EVP's of what she captured. We discussed some of the history and thoughts about what was happening out there, and I told her I would love to come out.

The day finally came when I could make it out and I brought a medium friend of mine along and we did a preliminary to get a feel for the house. Through that night, we got EMF fluctuations that were keying off of the questions I was asking Robert Caruso, the medium I had brought with me. These hits came in the living room when we first got there. In the first bedroom to the left of the living room, Robert had mentioned there was an elderly lady who was laying on the bed as he sat down; that room became 15 degrees colder than the ambient temperatures in the rest of home.

Robert and I decided to take a break from the sittings and went into the kitchen. We sat there for a little while and were discussing how the evening was going so far when we started hearing a male conversation in the back-right corner of the room. It was just loud enough to hear a male timbre to the voice and its cadence was unmistakably conversational. So, after we looked at each other I called for Martha, as she was there to help out Kathy in case, we needed anything. I asked her to stay with us because I had always wanted to work with her. We did another sitting and Robert pulled up some names and some ideas of who was doing the biting in the poker room. It was here that I saw the dark form of a child, about the size of a nine or ten year old, walk by the open curtain behind Martha. Robert and I both saw it and I think Martha felt something, honestly can't remember, but I know we all experienced the female child form, looking into the kitchen.

This night showed me that there is something happening at The Haunted Hill House, and that the reports I heard had some merit. I want to thank Kathy and Sonny Estes for allowing me to come out and look at things and I look forward to documenting more in the future. The book you will be reading is very well documented and the events thoroughly researched. I thank my friend Martha and I am honored to have been a part of this fine book…Enjoy Haunted Hill House…It is one of a kind.

Peter James Haviland A.C.C.H.

President of Lone Star Spirits Paranormal Investigations

Shelly Fisher

My husband Greg and I first saw Haunted Hill House when we went on a Ghost tour in Mineral Wells in July 2018 with some friends for my birthday. It was at the end of our tour and the group walked to the lot across the street from HHH. The tour guide told us very little about the house but said you could call and schedule a tour with the owners. I was instantly drawn to the house and researched it when we got home. I remember seeing the house on the news around Halloween time a few years before when it was for sale.

The owners Kathy and Sonny had only owned the property a few months when I scheduled a tour that august 2018. I couldn't wait to see the inside and hear all the stories. I had no idea what was waiting for us. I am a healthy skeptic, and this was the first time I experienced paranormal activity at a location that I could not explain away. Greg did not want to go and was on guard the entire time. He kept saying "I don't like this!" but I couldn't get enough.

At one point we were in Toby's room with Sonny looking at the SLS towards the door in front of the stairs. Sonny said a lady had told them that there were two bound demons on either side of the door. Sure enough using the SLS camera it mapped out two large figures on either side of the door. I wanted to debunk the SLS, so I walked over and stood beside the door on the right side where the stick figure was being mapped. Almost daring something to touch me and suddenly my hair got pulled. I had it up in a bun and I thought since the ceiling was sloped perhaps, I caught it on the wood slant but I was a good foot away from it. Greg even said I was too far away to have got it caught on the ceiling and he didn't want to be in the house any longer. After the tour we were outside visiting with Kathy. She showed me a cigarette being burned as she held it out beside her. It looked if someone was taking a drag from it, there was no wind, the tip lit up bright and smoke was coming from the filter side. She said it was Shadowman and that he likes to smoke. Kathy asked Greg if he wanted to get a rock thrown at him and since he felt "safe" outside the house he said sure. Greg walked beside the cars down the driveway and felt a rock hit the back of his right arm and he hurried back to us. Sonny and Kathy stayed late visiting with us and sharing stories.

I went to many public investigations with different paranormal teams after that experience, almost every month at the beginning of 2019. Others had experiences and I enjoyed hearing about them and seeing evidence on the DVR. It was a few months before I had another personal experience. Kathy and I talked about it. She said I may be a neutralizer. I'm very calm and don't get overly excited or jumpy when things happen, and I think some of the spirits at HHH prefer people that react and get scared easily. The next experience I had was when Greg and I were in the Carousel room, and I decided to do my first ever Facebook live. By this time, I had invested in my own paranormal equipment. We had our K2 and motion activated "cat balls". I asked questions and was getting yes/no responses. Then our responses stopped, and I could hear other investigators screaming and running down the stairs. There was another time it was the next morning and all the guests and investigators had left from the overnight. Kathy and Sonny allowed my husband and I to investigate on our own for a bit. We went upstairs into the Bootleggers room with a pinwheel and conducted another Facebook live. The window was open and there was a slight breeze, but we were asking questions and getting responses appropriately. But for some reason in my skeptical mind, I still didn't feel like I was communicating with the other side. That is until, Kathy had me use the bionic ears one morning after an event. I sat on the arm of the couch downstairs outside of the Shadowman's room with the doors all closed. I shut my eyes, placed the mic to the bottom of the door and heard a thud. I looked up to tell her I heard something, and she pointed and the door had opened right next to me. I stared through the crack and spoke very softly and got an ice cold breeze on my hand closest to the door. I had a very sad maternal feeling that overwhelmed me. Then it gradually went away. We went to check the DVR and you could see a white mist come from the cracked door and over my left hand. So having a personal, emotional and physical experience and also seeing something manifest at the exact same time on the DVR...... was amazing!

Our most recent visit was Halloween 2020. We stayed the night in the Bootleggers room on a blowup mattress. Greg and I talked about how the house felt very calm all night. Later that night we laid down to get a few hours sleep and Greg woke me up because the girl on the rocking horse started going off and it scared him. When the sun came up and Greg heard people in the kitchen, he decided it was safe enough to go down stairs. While Greg was gone, I was in and out of sleep and I felt a presence rush towards the doorway. It happened a few times, but I was so sleepy I didn't even react.

 It's awesome to see how the house has become more alive over time and how the owners have learned more and more about the history and the spirits of the house.

Greg has an overall bad feeling every visit but there has only been a couple of times I felt nauseous, headache and like I couldn't breathe when I visited. And those times I left early but I always returned. I only go when I'm in a positive frame of mind and I only bring positivity when I investigate.

I feel like I left a lot out. I've been to the house probably a half a dozen times or so. I was trying to focus on the most memorable events. After I sent the email, I remembered a couple of other experiences. The first overnight I spent there; I didn't really have any personal experiences. But I wasn't myself for three days after. My head was foggy, I felt irritable and depressed. I assumed it was lack of sleep at first but not after a couple of more days. I decided to sage the house and myself and do a prayer meditation. After that I felt a heaviness lifted and back to myself. I've never experienced that before, and it was my first time using sage. I have an EVP of a loud growl when Kathy enters the room. After I heard the growl and I remember that moment very well and there was no growl that was audible at the time. It kinda scared me. So, I have yet to go through hours of recordings and photos.

I've had two other SLS experiences I wanted to share. Both were late 2018 or early 2019 because I was still figuring out how the equipment worked and questioning the validity of the equipment. I was by myself in the rooms so no one else could verify what I was seeing. In the scratcher room I had the SLS, and was asking a stick figure to get close to the REM pod (I think, it was a motion activated device anyway) and make it go off. It looked like the stick figure moved over to where the REM pod was, sat in the chair next to it and was moving its arm to trigger it but nothing happened. So, I kept asking and it was almost like it got frustrated. It looked like it levitated above the REM pod and was trying to stomp on it with its foot. I laughed about what I was seeing then it disappeared and never came back. The other time was in Toby's room I had the SLS, and it mapped the two demons on either side of the doorway. I was asking for them to raise a hand to verify they were intelligent and validation that the SLS was mapping spirits and not just a flat wall. The one on the right side of the door looked like it put a noose around its neck and hung himself. I felt like I was watching a smart ass ghost from the movie Beetlejuice lol. I of course laughed because I was in disbelief that just happened. I asked several more times to do something. But it just stayed like that... arm in the air and head titled over. Still kind of makes me giggle.

I'm so drawn to HHH and I'm not sure if it's because it's the first place where I truly experienced paranormal, because everyone I have met there has been so friendly and open about paranormal discussions ......or is it the evil/negative entities that are tricking me to be drawn to the house.

Nikki Clark

I visited Hill House June of 2020. Didn't experience much until we went to bed. We stayed in the room that had the closed off bathroom....shadow man's room. I kept seeing a shadow move around. My friend was knocked out and we were both laying on our stomachs. I was awake the whole time and felt the top comforter be thrown off the bed. Something grabbed my foot and lifted my leg off the bed and continued to mess with my foot. This happened a few times. After that ended, something started whispering in my ear, doors started slamming and you could hear footsteps upstairs.

Sheena Lanham

My very first night there I had something breathe very hard into my right ear while in the carousal room. Sonny caught a lot of EVPs talking about my sister in law, her daughter and son in law. They were not nice things either. They said things like "cut her", "kill her", "he's a dick". The next morning Kathy was using the portal app and was talking to the spirits, showing us how it works, and she asked if someone could name a person in the kitchen. Shadow Man said my name, which blew me away because my name is very unusual. After I had been home a couple of days, I looked at all my pics I had taken and caught several things like, orbs, a large white misty figure outside next to Kathy.

My most eventful experience was with you in the Axe Room. We had just went to bed, around 3:00 in the morning, and it was all quite in the house. I heard a noise upstairs as if someone was moving furniture. Then there were 6-7 steps coming down the stairs, they sounded like old hard soled men shoes and then for about 2 seconds I heard children laughing at the foot of the stairs. I did not have any of my recording equipment, with me so I started videoing with my cell phone. I could not see what I was videoing, I did not want to move and wake you us. So, after a week or so after I had gotten back home I began looking through my pics and videos and then I seen it! A shadow figure began forming in the bedroom doorway. It slowly gets bigger, changes shape and stays there for about 15 - 20 minutes.

Just last Friday (9/20/19) I was at the Hill House around 5:00 visiting with Kathy and Sonny. Kathy had gotten a new toy for the children spirits. We were in the living room sitting on the sofa next to the door to Shadow Man's room. Kathy was asking her doll Lisa to play with the new toy and then seen Shadow Man's door open about 2-3 inches. So, I started recording. It was the coolest thing!!! I've seen videos of it but never in person. She asked who it was and said "when I say your name and you are the one that opened the door, shut the door so we will know it's you". She went through all the names and when she said "Joshua" the closed to about half an inch. She asked him if wanted to come out and play with the new toy, and he shut the door. She asked him to open it again and he did. But every time she asked him to come and play he would shut it. I got it all on video. That door sticks when you open or shut it, so he had to use some energy to do what he was doing.

Debbie Willard

I am Kathy's aunt Debbie. I have been to the HHH several times. I have also stayed overnight at the house. The following is my most memorable experience at the house....

Shortly after Kathy & Sonny had bought the house, I took my mom

(Kathy's grandmother, Mary) to the house to see it. Kathy was giving a tour that evening with some young ladies that were about to be college bound and suggested we come a little early so she could give my mom and I a private tour before she got busy with the girls that were coming. I believe the lady working with Kathy at the time was named Kara.

Mom & I arrived about 6:30 pm and I believe it was on a Thursday. Kathy gave us a walk thru of the downstairs and the outside. When we were in the "Scratcher Room" we sat at the table. It was hot in the room at the time. I think it was sometime in June. Kathy made the comment she felt something at her leg. We didn't see anything. I took some pictures and nothing showed up in the pictures I took. I had asked Kathy what the doors led to as I was trying to get my bearings of where I was in the house. One door was a small closet. The other door opened into the living room. However, at the time there was a couch on the other side of the door. We continued our quick tour with Kathy thru the rest of the downstairs. The ladies for the tour arrived as scheduled. There were three of them. Mom and I stayed pretty much in the kitchen with Sonny and Albert to not be "in the way" and we watched the monitors. This was all new to us. It was quite fascinating to see the orbs in the rooms. When the group tour headed for the scratcher room, Kathy invited me to step out on the front porch to take a smoke break with her. One of the ladies in the tour "quit" she was feeling very uneasy when they got to the scratcher room. She joined my mom & Sonny in the kitchen to watch monitors. Mom and the lady from the group wore headsets and could hear everything in the scratcher room. Kara came out on the porch for a smoke break too. She said the remaining two ladies were scared but were in the scratcher room alone. Kathy said I could join them if I wanted to. I went in the scratcher room with them. It was no longer daylight. It was dark. There was a candle lit on the table. The three of us sat there for a bit. One of the ladies was sitting in the same chair Kathy had sat in earlier and said she felt something around her leg. Again, we saw nothing. The flame on the candle would move almost like there was wind in the room - there was none. There was almost no air flow and it was hot. I heard loud, heavy footsteps. Almost like someone stomping. Then I heard chains, like heavy chains. I asked the two ladies if they heard them too. They did. The footsteps and chains sounded like they were coming from the door that opened into the living room. I thought maybe Albert was on the other side of the door stomping and shaking chains. He wasn't!!! We left the room and Sonny played back the video recordings. We could see all the orbs flying around us in the room. My mom and the other lady heard the chains thru the headsets. They assured us it was not Albert on the other side of the door. The monitors also showed it was not Albert.

I had been waiting to go upstairs since before the ladies arrived! My mom has some difficulty walking so she did not join us upstairs. Sonny gave us (the three ladies and myself) a tour of the upstairs and Albert & Kara joined us. It was extremely hot upstairs and very dusty. As we entered the room at the top of the stairs and walked in, the walls on each side of the door growled at me. No one else heard it. It was a very evil satanic growl. It made me very uncomfortable. Sonny & the three ladies & Kara sat in the floor in the little room upstairs with the window above the street. They were attempting to make contact with the spirits in the house. I stood with Albert in the doorway. Again, it was extremely hot and no air movement. All of a sudden, a ball came rolling across the floor from the room behind me. It stopped once it hit the wall. I watched it come to a complete stop and a few seconds later it rolled a different direction! I was still feeling very uncomfortable from the walls growling at me. I was also getting extremely hot and I went back downstairs. When the group came downstairs we gathered in the living room with the loud portal box trying to contact spirits. I sat on the couch with one of the ladies from the group. The door going to the scratcher room was behind us. I heard a man's voice behind me say "These damn chains"! The other lady heard it too! She asked if she could use my flashlight to check her leg. She was bleeding. We went in the kitchen where it was well lit. She had a large scratch on her leg. This was the lady sitting in the same spot Kathy had been in (The scratcher room) and they both had made the comment they felt something by their leg. Kathy and Sonny said it looked like the lady may have been scratching her leg upstairs on the recordings they watched. The lady insisted she hadn't and did not have any mosquito bites either.

I have been to the house numerous times since. I still feel very uncomfortable when I have been upstairs and I prefer not to go upstairs. When I do go upstairs I take Holy Water with me! I have taken friends to

the house, some are very skeptical and they have not experienced anything. Like I told them, I can only tell them what I have experienced. Believe me or not it's up to them, it is what I have experienced!

Kathy & Sonny as you know have grown tremendously since when they first bought the house. They have a lot of equipment that I never mess with when I am there (I really don't know how to use that stuff) They are both Christian, honest and loving people. I am a little bias, as I love them both. But I know they would not lie to me. I know my experience was real in the house. I know what I heard, what I felt, and what I saw!

A photograph of my bite and scratch several days after it happened.

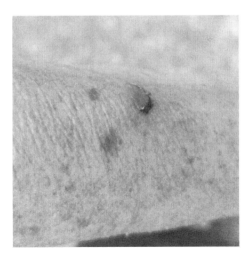

HOW HAUNTED HILL HOUSE HAS
INTERACTED WITH ME

I have been coming to this house quite a bit the past three years. A lot had to do with conducting research for this book. That included staying overnight quite a bit all in the name of research. It was and is still research as there are more books to come. My friend, Maria Elana Santos Kempf, introduced me to Haunted Hill. Since the initial encounter I have become close friend with Kathy and Sonny. The house seems to know when I am on my way to visit. This has been discovered through some of the unsolicited EVPS the Estes obtain on their security camera system. Some have said, "Martha's coming. Martha's here. It's Martha. I love Martha." I know, it seems nuts.

As a retired detective and as a journalist, I came to the house with an unbiased mind and let the evidence show itself. I didn't know much about the house other than it was by the Baker Hotel and was alleged to be haunted. I didn't know the history or how many murders, old and recent had occurred at the house and on the lot next door. There used to be a house on that lot. The Estes' are still trying to research their property on East Mountain behind the house. I have been up that mountain with a walking stick and a metal detector. It's a really tough climb. The big cacti are huge with trunks the size of tree trunks. Then there is the jumping cactus, snakes and large boulders. The mountain is off limits to house visitors in general because it is rugged, and the Estes' are concerned about visitor safety.

I have stayed overnight in the house a number of times. Never have I left in the middle of the night or slept on the porch or under the kitchen table. Many of the times I was there alone. Sometimes totally alone and other times Sonny and Kathy were outside in the camper. Initially, I stayed in a hotel. Eventually I agreed to stay in the house. My first visits to the house told my gut not to stay in it. That was the first year they bought the house. By the winter my gut told me it would be okay to stay in the house.

The time was October. Sonny and Kathy had purchased the house a few months earlier. Someone started running a Halloween haunted house inside the haunted house. I could feel the house becoming charged. You could feel the electricity and the excitement from within. It was almost as if the house was ready and anxiously awaiting all the energy it would absorb from the terror of those getting scared as they moved room to room inside the downstairs of the house. The negativity grew stronger. It was if a few of the negative entities were feeding off people who came and were scared. Then there was the energy of the young children.

Several people felt the energy becoming stronger with each walk through and tour. As the good energy in the house seemed too temporarily dim, the negative energy was sucking up everything it could. Besides the Halloween scary wander through the house there were tours. The tours consisted of a docent in each downstairs room to tell the history and explain a variety of tools used by paranormal investigators. Every once in a while, there will be tours like this in the house. To care for and protect the home the tours were cut drastically by the owners who feel as they are the caretakers for the house. The tour events usually include only the downstairs. Maybe once a year a tour will occur where the upstairs rooms are included. They don't want to tax the house facilities with too many visitors.

The first time I was at the house there was an event aka tour. I was assigned to the Scratch Room. Kathy told me there were 75 documented scratches in that room and showed me pictures. Being polite I listened but was thinking, "Sure." I can tell you that evening a few hundred people came through the room. I witnessed about 24 scratches which occurred in various groups. While some could be self-made by scratching themselves out of site, I watched as scratches formed on a number of people. That means their arm was out, or their neck, and a red mark down the arm or neck formed with 6-10 people watching each time. There were several teenage males in one group who seemed to border on delinquent by their behavior. They got in because it was thought they were with some of the adults. Turned out they were not. When they walked through the bathroom in the Axe Room on their way to the Passage Room and on into the Scratcher Room one or two got a big scratch on their neck. Then while they were in the Scratcher Room they got scratched again. Turned out they also stole a book that was on the living room coffee table and tried to steal the jar where people had put in tip money from a ghost walk earlier that night. Since then, it has seemed that the house or spirits know a bad apple when it comes to the house. Often that person may end up dealing with negative activity during their visit. If someone comes to the house with bad intentions, they will probably experience activity, but it may not be welcome. Then there are those who bring their own attachments with them to the house. They may not even realize they have the attachment. It seems the house knows and often reacts to it.

Some attachments may stay at the house while things from the house may leave with a guest unbeknownst to them until later. I have been at the house when Kathy has received phone calls from someone who had recently been at the house. They will say something followed them home. Kathy talks to the person and will talk to the spirit through the speaker. Most the time it seems the spirit returns if it was ever gone. Otherwise, it at least gives the person good peace of mind. Then there are the visitors who have had to return to the house and bring spirit back. It doesn't happen often, but it does happen. Most aren't thrilled when they think the Shadowman chose to come home with them. Shadowman isn't very nice. Sometimes it's a child spirit.

One thing Kathy tries to do with all visitors before they leave is to pray over them, anoint them with holy oil and then does the same with their vehicle. It seems it's the people who choose not to have this done later discover something has followed them home.

I have been scratched, bitten, growled at, and hissed at, watched doors open and close. I have heard the piano keys play, heard audible voices, and recorded electronic voice phenomena. I have seen orbs emitting their own light with my eyes. I have felt the presence of negative and positive energy. I have felt the energy when it comes into my own space and then when it leaves. I have seen shadows, apparitions and other unidentified things in the house. The energy I felt in the past during many investigations would feel positive, negative, male or female. I have felt it like that for many years. I could often tell when it came and when it left. Now, after being in the house a number of times I feel it in a different manner. It changed a couple years ago. I feel this not only at HHH but during other investigations. While there are cold spots all over different places, this is different. I can even be in a different location talking about the house and suddenly someone or thing from the house is there. The feeling I get is more than cold. It's as if someone just poured a cooler full of ice water, with the ice, on top of me. It's more than goosebumps. It can move around so that it's behind me, on one side or another and can completely engulf my entire body. It's a very strong feeling.

I think I may have learned how to open more here than anywhere. It was something difficult for me to re-learn after closing it down so deep for all the years I was in law enforcement even though I used some of it at times.

I remember talking to Teal Gray once during an event. We were nowhere near Mineral Wells but were talking about the children of Haunted Hill House. Suddenly we look at each other and smile in a knowing way. The children were with us. We could feel the energy surrounding us as we talked and acknowledged them. When the subject was changed, the children were gone. This happens quite often to me. But just with this house. The only other time I get this feeling is if I'm in a location and talking about someone who may have lived at that location. It lets me know I am on the right track. Especially if a mystery is involved such as an unsolved murder.

I have done different things when at the house to see if it elicits any response. A few visits have included sitting on the living room floor and reading a book to the children as if they were there. I will visualize the children sitting anxiously at my feet waiting to see which story I am about to read. There hasn't been much of a reaction as far as I know, but that doesn't mean the reading didn't affect something. I'm not the only one reading to the children.

Now there are several of us who read.

I remember leaving one day and I turned toward the living room while walking out the back door. I had turned to say goodbye to the children and that I would return. The overhead light in the living room flickered several times as if to say goodbye. That was interesting as it seemed to be a direct response to what was said.

It's interesting to listen to the EVP's obtained through the home's security system. Some of them have said, "Martha's here. Martha's coming. It's Martha." The interactions with people continue to amaze me. There have been plenty of other comments made by spirits about people visiting the house and about the owners. Some are downright hilarious while others have been rather snarky. One of the books in this series while be strictly about the paranormal and the interactions between people at the house and with the owners. I will touch lightly on it here but the bulk with be in the paranormal edition of the book.

One of the days I was there four of us were in the living room, including Kathy, Donna McCauley, myself and Julie Hester. Kathy had noticed that when nursery rhymes were sung in the kitchen the door leading into the Shadowman Room would open. It appeared that one of the boys had moved into the passage room between the living room and the Shadowman Room. Kathy found the child seemed to like and interact with little red truck toys. She would play with one that you could roll back, winding it up, and then it would roll forward on its own. The door would slowly open. Then it started happening with nursery rhymes.

On this day we tried any number of nursery rhymes, and nothing worked. That is until we began to sing, "Duck, duck, goose." Kathy was sitting on the arm up a couch that was by the door to the Shadowman Room. After we sang the chant, Kathy would stand up and slowly run around the coffee table. As she ran the door into that room would swing open. We were thinking it may have been Joshua as he had started coming downstairs. Once this happened Kathy would stop and tell him if he wanted to play again to shut the door and it would slowly close. It stayed closed until we sang it again. We did this about six times. Each time the door would open and then slowly closed when Kathy asked for it to shut. It was an amazing experience.

There was something which showed up at the house and hadn't been there before. It feels very tall and slim. It stands in the corner between the front door and the door to the Axe Room. This is at the bottom of the stairs. I have felt it and it makes my skin crawl. Yet, I still continue to sleep in the Axe Room and will continue to stay in that room when possible.

One night I was sleeping in the house alone in the Axe Room. This is one of my earliest nights to stay there alone. Kathy and Sonny were in the camper in the backyard. I was sleeping on the side of the bed by the bottom of the stairs and the front door. The door from the hall to the living room was open. I like to do this so I can hear anything that might go on in the house. I hear a lot when I do this, a lot. It's both residual and intelligent. It was around 4:00 AM when I was awakened by a loud, "Bam, bam, bam" on the piano keys. The piano is in the living room. It sounded like a child had taken a hand and pounded down on a group of keys at the same time. I woke up, listened and then went back to sleep. I felt grateful to have heard this happen.

It doesn't happen a lot, but others have heard it. Often, it's only one key in the higher range. That "ting" has startled a few people, including Kathy. If you remember what the former resident told me during the interview it was happening when they lived in the house. She said the piano used to be in her bedroom. She moved it into the living room because she got tired of the keys getting played in the middle of the night. It would keep her up and was good at waking her if she was asleep.

Something which shouldn't surprise me is what has happened a number of times while writing this book. A lot of the writing is done late at night, and I will visualize what I write about. As I do I get the feeling the house knows I'm writing about it and something from it will show up and wrap itself around me, like it is right now. It started at my feet swirling around my legs, up to my torso and on and on up until it's wrapped around my head. Can't say if it's good or bad. It doesn't scare or unnerve me. I have gotten used to the feeling. Other times it comes in hard and cold and slams completely around me like a blanket coming straight out of the freezer.

Now then, Toby is another story. I was asleep one night in the Axe Room. I woke to a growl in my ear. It was loud enough to wake me but not enough to scare me. Did I run screaming out of the house? No. I ignored it and went back to sleep. Yes, I did. I went right back to sleep. I think my father prepared me for this when I was a child. He loved to hide and then jump out and roar hoping to see the little girls scream and run. All of them did except for me. Now jumping and growling usually doesn't cause me to even bat an eye. Being in law enforcement helped as well. I had to be prepared for the unexpected, so it takes a lot to make me jump or flinch. I remember Sonny has tried many times to scare me. I just look at him. But he did get me once. I jumped a little bit. It was hilarious and he was extremely pleased with himself.

When the growl that woke me up didn't elicit a response it didn't satisfy Toby. During another overnight I was again alone in the Axe Room. This time just as I was getting settled and closing my eye. You know the feeling, you ease into a comfy bed and think, ahhh. I heard a loud growl. I had barely closed my eyes. It seemed so close that if I had opened my eyes, Toby and I would have been nose to nose. It felt like the growl blew my hair back and I could almost feel the spittle from the growl. Reminded me of a child trying to get your attention. If one thing doesn't work, they try a different tactic. I didn't want to see eye to eye at that time. If I had opened my eyes there probably would have been a reaction to Toby. Nope, not going to give Toby any satisfaction. My eyes remained closed, and I went to sleep without acknowledging the growl. That wouldn't be the end of it.

Toby made sure I would react months later. I'll tell more soon.

An event was going on one summer and a number of people were in the house investigating. Priscilla's room was a covered porch. Now it's a beautiful bedroom with a bath and spirits. A group of people were in the Shadowman Room and Marie Davis was using dowsing rods in an attempt to speak with Shadowman. It seemed there may have been something negative in the room for a bit. It left the room. I was in there and decided to go outside and talk with Kathy and Maria for a few minutes. I went out the backdoor and ran through the pouring rain and onto the covered porch. Kathy and Maria commented when I came in that there had been a negative energy on the porch with them until I walked in. They said that as I came in the energy went into the Shadowman Room. We started noticing a pattern of this after I had talked to John Zaffis about how negative energy seems to stop after people call me concerned about their location and ask for help. When I start to arrange visiting their homes all activity would suddenly stop. Zaffis told me it was because I was a neutralizer. Something I had never thought about but wondered why this happened. I still don't know much about being a neutralizer. Yet there is still activity when I am around. After talking to Kathy and Maria I went back into the house through the rain and got a little wet. I went to the Shadowman Room. Everyone was still there, and Marie was still using dowsing rods. I held up my phone using the flashlight so they could see any response or movement of the rods.

After a while my arm got tired. I sat down on the edge of the bed. As I did, I felt what I thought was water from the rain on my arm. I started to wipe it off with my other hand and it was thicker than water. Everyone in the room looked at my arm as I shined a light on it. There was blood dripping down my arm to my elbow. Quite a bit in fact. I went to the kitchen. A number of people were there and saw all the blood. I went to get something to clean it and wipe off the blood. A few people helped with the cleanup. The scratch on my arm looked like someone had taken a fingernail and peeled back the skin. It was 1-2 inches long. The scratch was cleaned, some of the skin was pulled back up and it was covered after I took a photo. It never hurt. I never felt the skin peel back. Nor did I see or feel a bite. Several days later I was outside, and the sun hit the scratched area just right. It was then I saw the bite marks. They were in a perfect circle around the area of the scratch. There were indentions in the skin. It looked like tiny pointy sharp teeth, yet they never broke the skin. I got a good photo of that. The photo is included in the book. The one scratch turned into the big one and two smaller marks so they looked like a smiley face on my arm with teeth circling them. Most people know I'm not big on smiley face icons.

This was the second time someone was bitten like this at the house. A frequent visitor, Albert had the same scratch and smiley face. I think later there was a third person with the same smiley face. Another odd thing the Kathy has taken note of is that many of those getting scratched or bit have Type O blood. Mine is O negative. They have EVPS taken off the security cameras where something mentions needing to feed by biting. They have more than one EVP with such comments. Creepy.

Missing Time

That wasn't all that happened to me that night. It seems, according to several people, I had missing time. I am not the only person who has lost time in the house. I was told after the scratch I disappeared for about an hour and no one knew where I went. Then about the time they started to look for me I came out of the Shadowman Room. There are cameras all over the house and no one could see me in the cameras. I have no memory of this other than going into a room for a bit and coming out. Kathy said she did see me at one point, and I was deep into something on my phone, but I don't remember being on my phone. I'm not one to have it attached to my hand or have it growing out of my face. They said I seemed disoriented when I came into the living room. I wasn't aware of any missing time. I was able to account for the time but was told I hadn't done what I said I did as if I had a false memory of the time. There does seem to be portals in the house. Maybe I found one. Who knows what happened? So far this is the only missing time I have had at the house. At least I don't know of any other time, but I have spent quite a bit of time inside the house alone.

One day I was walking through the living room toward the kitchen. I don't remember if I was the only one inside. The front door and the back door were closed. There was no breeze inside and no open windows. The door from the living room to the hall by the kitchen was open. The doors to all the rooms that are accessed through the living room were closed. As I approached the open door leading to the hallway and kitchen it swiftly swung closed. I stopped in my tracks and looked around thinking that was sort of cool. I turned around to a sound and watched the door to the Scratcher Room open. I stood there with a wide gaping mouth looking from door to door. I acknowledged what happened and waited for an audible response. When none came, I opened the closed door and went into the kitchen to get whatever it was I wanted and went back outside. I didn't feel threatened. I don't know the point of the doors opening and closing, unless something thought it would scare me.

Around the end of 2020 there was a group at the house. I brought a 432 MHz A note singing bowl. Another person and I went upstairs with the bowl. We went into Toby's Room and sat on the floor. A singing bowl hadn't been used in the house before, so it was an experiment. I got the bowl singing loud for several minutes. We had it on the HHH Facebook Live feed. Then I let it wind down. The whole house seemed to vibrate with the energy coming from the singing bowl. The house could feel it in the walls and everyone there felt it in their bones. Once the sound and vibrations stopped, we (upstairs) asked the spirits if they liked the sound. There was an audible yes, but we also got several resounding no's and a few audible growls and hisses. Sounded like Toby wasn't happy. Later that evening we went back upstairs and sat Emily's Room. We were asking questions again and got several EVP responses. However, we started getting several louder and more aggressive growl and hisses. They sounded like they were coming from Toby's room. This was the most growls and hisses that I have ever heard during one visit. They went from being low to sounding more aggressive. I will use the bowl more often now at the house. We decided it was time to calmly get our stuff and head downstairs. Now I usually bring the bowl with me in case I want to try another session. I have a turning fork I bring along as well.

Maria and I were staying in the camper several nights while we were holding an event in the house. Maria was in the bedroom, and I was on a very comfortable couch. The camper would shake during the night. Not a lot but enough to notice. I thought it was Maria wiggling around on the bed trying to get comfortable. The shaking is something that has happened a number of times I have stayed in the camper. I never said anything to Maria that night. It happened again the second night. The next morning, I said something to Maria. She said she wasn't moving and thought it was me. I hadn't been moving. We both thought the other was the culprit. The culprit may have been the Shadowman. Kathy has said a number of times that when she is in the camper alone the Shadowman shakes it. Now I know what she meant. It has happened nearly every time I have stayed in the camper. Even when Kathy and Sonny are in the camper. Those were the times I thought it was Sonny wiggling around.

Experiences happen in the house, the yard and on the empty lot. More than one would expect. One year a paranormal military group that used to stay often were building a maze on the empty lot for Halloween. One of the guys had a brick thrown at him. The brick had been laying on the ground by HHH with a bunch of other bricks. No one was outside on the side yard at the house when it happened. Other things have happened to him. I will go into more detail when I publish the paranormal book in the series.

K athy and Sonny were kind enough to give me the house for a bit as a research experiment. They don't live in the house. It had been a number of years since anyone lived in the house. I spent two nights and three days alone in the house one September. I wanted to stay and act like I was living there. I wanted to experience what type of interactions may occur. I was there from Sunday afternoon until Tuesday afternoon. Toby did get me good during the stay.

While there I took note of anything I noticed, and I will document it here. It was fairly calm until the second night. So here goes.....

Sunday September 22

2:30 PM - I arrive at the house. While I had already spent a number of nights alone in the house. This had a different feeling. It was with a bit of trepidation I wandered on inside the house. Kathy and Sonny hadn't left yet. They had planned on being gone by the time I arrived.

4:30 PM – I left to go to Walmart to pick up a few things and grab a meal at the Chinese fast food place. I get back, eat and start to set up my computer and a few other things. I lay out any documents I may need as I planned to work on this book while at the house. I connect to the TV and turn on my computer. The house is extra-ordinarily calm. That makes me a little leery for when the night comes to visit. Several hours later I eat dinner. The other was a late lunch. Dinner was leftovers from lunch. I spend time doing some research for the book while watching some TV. I make a few phone calls and it's still calm and quiet. Too quiet.

6:32 PM – The door leading into the back of Joshua's room opens. I didn't notice it until the next day. That was odd because I was watching the cameras when I was in the kitchen.

7:30 PM – I begin to hear noises in the hall. I was sitting at the kitchen table on the end closest to the hall and faced the hall. I didn't want to put my back to the doorway. I still don't like to do that and will face the door. The sounds were coming from the hall near the bottom of the stairs and by the Axe Room. These weren't the residua sounds I'm used to hearing. This went on for about 30 minutes. I heard the sounds off and on. Some were creaks in the floorboards, and some may have been on the stairs. I didn't see anything on the security cameras either. However, right now as I write this, I am hearing sounds in my bedroom that shouldn't be present. The dog is barking outside by the bedroom window. Rather unnerving again since my back is to the sounds.

7:54 PM – I'm still in the kitchen and watched an orb go past in the hall. I saw it with my eyes and not on the cameras. The hairs all over started to stand up. Right now, that ice cold feeling I get is creeping around me while I try to shake it off. Does that mean the house is curious? I happened to be watching the Strangetown episode that was done at HHH soon after the Estes' bought the house. Some of the information mentioned on that episode changed after the research Kathy and Donna have done on the house.

7:58 PM – Now I hear someone walking upstairs. Only I am still alone in the house. I'm used to this sound. It's both residual and at times intelligent. There is a lot more residual upstairs when it comes to walking.

8:30 PM – I took a break and called my husband. Then I watched a little "normal" TV.

9:15 PM – I was actually read for bed. That's unusual because my normal crash time at the house is around 3:30 AM. That's even a struggle because I seem to get energized at the house. So much so that when I end up with a mere three hours of sleep, I will feel like it's been at least eight hours. The house is still calm. I watch some more TV while working on the book.

10:50 PM – I decided to settle in for the night. Of course, I stayed in the Axe Room. At this time, I would sleep on the side of the bed closest to the door so I could hear things in the house. Yep, even though I was alone. But then, I wasn't really ever alone. The spirits of the house were right there with me the entire time. Like I would really be falling asleep by 11:00 PM. Right now, you should fall out of your chair because that's such a hilarious idea.

11:40 PM – I heard a really loud pop or bang. It sounded like something was thrown at the front door. I was not going to unlock the door and investigate. I could have been a live person trying to see if anyone was inside. No thank you ma'am. Besides I didn't have a gun with me in the house. This is Texas and I do carry a weapon. If you went alone to as many places in the middle of nowhere you might think about doing the same. I think on this night I was asleep by midnight. I slept all night. Nothing woke me up.

Monday, September 23

7:00 AM – I woke up to the sound of a male voice. It sounded German. It was a deep voice. I heard one word but couldn't discern what was said since I don't speak much. As a side note, Kathy found a German World War II helmet at a shop and brought it to HHH. The helmet lights up EMF devices. This wasn't the first time German was heard in the house. It wasn't until the helmet was brought in that German started showing up on EVPS and disembodied voices. This is what I heard. I was still the lone person inside the house. I went outside on the front porch to see if I could find anything that may have hit the house or thrown at the house. I couldn't find anything.

The German helmet can be found on the bookcase in the Scratcher Room. On the opposite side of the Axe room from the door is a bathroom. The door doesn't quite seal shut. Then there is a door into the Passage Room from the bathroom. That door won't close all the way. On the other side of the small Passage Room is another door to the Scratcher Room. It had a window on the top half of the door. It was broken out several years ago when a visitor got scared and tried to leave in a hurry. She smashed the window. It's an antique door possibly original to the house. There is a towel covering the opening. I think Kathy's afraid someone else might try to get out of that room in a hurry and again break the window. I've tried EVP session where I try to establish communication by stating I'm German. I do have German blood. It's also where the Hazzard came from in my name. A number of people have heard German in the house since the helmet was introduced.

11:24 AM – I spoke to Kathy via text just before then. It's still too quiet in the house. I spend time working on my computer. Everything in the house begins to feel calm and comfortable. That should have been a: Here's your sign" moment.

1:00 PM – I went outside on the front porch for a relaxing break. I listened to the sounds of traffic and nature. When I went back inside, I saw the passage door in Joshua's room upstairs was open. It was closed the entire time I was there. I hadn't gone upstairs, and no windows were open. If there had been an open window and a breeze it would have shut the door. I went to the security cameras and went back to when it opened. That showed when it happened. It didn't look open to me at all the day before. Shows how something can happen in front of your eyes yet it goes unnoticed.

2:30 PM – I went upstairs for the first time on this visit to shut the door. If you haven't been inside the house, Joshua's room has a small door inside on the left. It's there to access the rest of the attic and to conduct paranormal exercises. Some people go back there to leave toys. Some to try and communicate with Joshua. Part of the fireplace chimney is in there. It doesn't go through the roof. Investigators have seen balls move on their own and picked up EVPS.

2:36 PM – I shut the small door in Joshua's room. I heard the door latch.

3:18 PM – I closed the door in Joshua's room again. This time I took a child's chair and placed it against the door so it would stay shut. This time the door wouldn't stay shut. The door can stay closed for weeks and then one day it opens. I have closed it in the past. Then I push on it, jump up and down and stomp. The door will remain closed. Not this time.

3:40 PM – I went to the living room, sat on the floor and read a couple children's stories out loud. This is pretty much the only thing I did that came close to investigating. I wanted to stir up some activity but didn't want to do and serious investigating during this stay. I wanted the dynamics to stay the same, as if I was living there and going about my daily routine. When done I went outside for a bit and spoke to my husband and a friend.

5:39 PM – I was inside and decided to eat dinner in the kitchen. I started to feel a little on edge as I was starting to feel the house energy building. I think I spent a lot of time in the kitchen during my stay. I had my computer and TV set up there. Now the TV is in the living room.

8:33 PM – My uneasiness really began to build. I have learned to trust my gut as I feel things and it's saved me a few times. I tried to shake the feeling, but it stayed strong. I started to feel shaky, and I began to get a rapid heartbeat. You know, like your heart is going to beat right out of your chest. I talked to Kathy a few minutes by phone. Worked on the book. Then I started to feel better. Like the danger had passed.

10:21 PM – I realized I was hearing music playing in the house. Only it wasn't. I heard the sound of a baby. Without realizing it I was humming to the music. Once I realized what I was doing and that there was music it stopped. That was a new one for me. Since then myself and others have heard a baby cry. That would make sense due to some of the past activity in the house. There may have been babies stolen and sold to rich people during the time of the brothel. The floorboards upstairs began to creak loud enough I could hear it in the kitchen.

11:11 PM – Interesting time for something to happen. I was completely calm and about to call it a night. That is until something crazy happened. I drove me out of the house to recover and calm down. It was very quiet. The TV was off, and I had just closed the laptop when it happened, and it happened with force. All of a sudden there was the LOUDEST hiss/roar/growl I have ever hear coming from upstairs. I can't really describe the sound well. Needless to say, it rather took me aback. Yes, it did startle me, a lot. I quickly got up from the table and ran to the kitchen door. While looking out and up I swung open the door to the living room. I didn't realize it was closed. I looked upstairs and hollered, "I heard you! What?" I did the same while looking into the living room. After the house stopped vibrating it was quiet again. I was pumped up and needed to calm down. I went to the front door and unlocked all the locks. I felt I needed to go outside to calm down. I called

Kathy while I was unlocking the door. I told her what happened. I had triggered one of the security cameras that has audio. Sonny looked and listened to it while I was on the phone. He said as I walked past the camera, he had an EVP that said, "Look! Toby made her turn red. He'll get her later." That worried Kathy. They called Julie Hester and asked her to come over. She lives about five minutes away. Her son, Ryan, came with her. We went inside. I told them not to investigate but to leave everything alone so energy wouldn't change. Shoot, my heart hurt, and I had shoulder pain. Others have felt their heart hurt at this house since then. They stayed for several hours and left while I was asleep.

Tuesday September 24
12:46 AM - Julie and Ryan sat in the Scratcher Room for a bit while I worked some more on my computer. I was now wide awake. I became calmer but my heart still hurt.
1:43 AM – Ryan was in the Shadowman room and saw or heard the toilet seat in the bathroom lift up and drop down.
2:41 AM – Ryan and Julie went upstairs. They took no equipment since I asked them not to investigate. Sitting anywhere was fine. I went to bed.
3:00 AM till 4: AM – I heard a mechanical music box begin to play. I also heard a male voice outside on the front porch around that time. I think Julie and Ryan had settled down. They were not outside on the front porch when I heard the voice. They were in the living room.
7:00 AM – I got up around this time and they were crashed in the living room.
10:00 AM – Julie and Ryan left. However, the way I remember it was I got up at 6:00 AM and they were gone. But my notes indicate the left around 10:00 AM. I'll go with that. Once I was alone, I began to hear talking. The kind you hear when people are talking but they are too far away for you to understand what's being said. Then there were creaks I was hearing from upstairs. The uneasy feeling returned. I got dressed and moving for the day. I watch TV during the day while I was going through several history books. I

was researching the house and was unable to find anything. Most old photographs don't have the house in them. It's weird.

I had gone upstairs when I was alone because once again, I saw the door in Joshua's room was open. As I reached the top of the stairs I looked into Toby's Room and asked him if he made the noise last night. I had triggered the security camera with audio as I reached the landing. I asked Toby if he was the one that made the noise the previous night. Sonny sent me the EVP and video. Almost as soon as I asked the question there was a direct response of, "Yep." It was in the voice most of us have learned to recognize as Toby. It's the type of voice you would expect to hear if a lizard or snake could talk.

I continued to Joshua's room. I went inside and shut the door. Now remember I had placed a chair against the door the day before. The chair was moved. I jumped around, banged on the wall and the door wouldn't open. When I got downstairs, I saw on the camera the door was open again. I went back upstairs and shut the door. This time it stayed shut. I backed up the DVR system to find when and how the door opened. I found it. Sometimes you can't find things that happen. It's as if that part was erased from the DVR system. I recorded the opening and me inside off their TV. I looked at it 5-6 times and then I saw it...

I watched me come into the room. Right behind are three dark shadows and all were of different heights. They come into the room with me. When I walk out of the room, I see the shadows turn and follow me. Those were the shadow figures of things not living in the house. I was on alert but not afraid.

2:00 PM – Kathy and Sonny arrived at the house. Sonny left a few minutes later while Kathy and I were in the kitchen talking. I planned to leave after Sonny returned. While talking we heard something new. We heard a loud voice coming from somewhere inside the house. We couldn't make put the word, but it was loud. It sounded just like Sonny. He wasn't there. It sounded like someone would sound if they were using an old time PA system. The voice was tinny sounding. We looked at each other. Then we made sure Sonny wasn't in the house. Kathy called Sonny. He was at the dollar store. Don't know where that came from, and I haven't heard it since.

Then we watched the door in Joshua's room open slowly, again. I went back upstairs and closed the door. I asked who was talking earlier to the air. There was no audible answer and no EVP response. I checked outside and there was no one around using a PA, bullhorn or speaker. Kathy and I spent some time looking around the house for something that could have made the mechanical sounding music I heard during the night. It wasn't Julie or Ryan. We couldn't find anything to make that noise where I could hear it. I left soon after. Since this time Kathy has heard the loud growly sound. One or two visitors have heard the sound. We are not sure from where it comes.

The House

This is quite the house. It's an enigma and an anomaly. There are a number of rooms and activity can almost always be found in one room or another. I will touch lightly on each room. I will start from the backyard. There will be more detail in future books .Portals to Hell filmed an episode at the house. Katrina had to leave the property at one point and Jack Osbourne had said during a number of interviews the house is the scariest place he has been. Some of the information in the episode on the house was wrong. They got some of the rooms mixed up. Before the crew began to film Jack was in the Shadowman Room. He stepped into the former sealed up bathroom and got touched. There was enough activity when Paranormal Declassified filmed here that Tim Wood has returned several times with friends. Each time the amount of activity blows them away. There have been other shows that filmed at the house. The most recent was Nick Groff for his new show Death Walker. It will be on Discovery Plus soon. Currently it's running in the UK. Other big shows have been turned down. Kathy doesn't want the house to be a mockery. She is interested in finding scientific evidence of what might be there. Kathy has added a large number of artifacts, antiques and dolls to the house. Some of the items and dolls are really active and downright spooky.

The camper outside

The camper gets rocked nearly every time someone stays out there. Just imagine being Phil. You're in your camper nice and calm when suddenly out of nowhere something you can't see slams into the side of your camper so violently you think it's going to tip the camper over with you inside. Your life probably flashes before you. That happened to Phil. The camper back there now is a different one. It still shakes, rattles and come close to rolling. Kathy has felt it shake a lot. She has had something slam up against it too many times. Maria and I have had the same experience. There's talk and I have felt from day one there is an accent entity in the backyard. It's a protector of something. Several of us feel it's Native American. They used to live in the area. The Shadowman comes outside and hangs out near the camper. I have seen some of the strangest things outside. One night a few years ago there was a group of us outside by the camper. Kathy had discovered Shadowman likes cigarettes and has smoked some of her cigarette. I thought she was nuts, sort of, when she told me that. Well, that was before I saw it happen with my own eyes. The cigarette was lit and held out. Shadowman was told he could take a drag off of it. We all watched the cigarette light up as it would if someone was taking a drag off it. We watched the cigarette glow and it quickly burned down. It was something I hadn't seen.

The Backyard, side yard and East Mountain

Many people have seen odd things in the yard toward "the hill." The Estes' may have seen a possible UFO by the hill. Once an empath asked to walk around the outside of the house. This was soon after they bought the house. Kathy put it on Facebook Live. One of the best EVPS I have heard came from the well area. No one was asking anything by the well. The EVP came in loud and clear. It said, "Help me." It sounded like a little boy. It said, "I'm scared" as well. There are two wells on the property by the house. They seem to be one of the first or second wells in the town. Deborah Rentfro used to live in the house with her sister and started drinking the water from the well. She claimed it cured her. After a few years there were 20 bathhouses and many wells. Judge J Lynch came into town and at one point ordered all the wells sealed. There is a well in the backyard and the house is built over a second well. A stream also flows deep under the house. The area has a lot of quartz. Water and quartz are two items that tend to be found where there is a lot of paranormal activity.

There is a story that a drunken cowboy fell into the well and died. They did pull him out of the well. Around the corner on the side of the house is a story where it is said Jacob died. He was tortured, murdered and possibly sexually abused. His death was made to look like an accident. He is not the only child murdered on this property .He was found on his swing, twisted in with the chains on his swing.

East Mountain was a hill with quite the reputation. When the bath houses were in their heyday people would walk up the mountain by steep steps. Others would ride a donkey to the top. The welcome sign for the city used to be on this mountain. There was a tower built over here for the Baker Hotel. Sonny, Donna and Gypsy from Zero Discrimination have found the footings for the sign. They have found part of the water tower and a lot of old trash from the Baker Hotel. The hotel has been closed for years. Baby jars with black sludge have been found on the hill not too far from the house. People often see beings or people in the back on the mountain or in the trees near the house. When Paranormal Declassified was filming they took a break a few people stepped outside. They saw a figure in the woods just off the backyard. They thought it was Sonny and waved. It wasn't Sonny. He was inside the camper with Kathy.

The Altar

In the backyard toward the woods is a creation partially built and partially using the rocks on the ground. Some people have claimed it was a BBQ pit. It wasn't and others claim it was used like an altar. I have said it looks like it could have been an opening to the tunnel system. It's just the right size for someone to walk out of from underground. No one has been able to figure it out yet. A neighbor once found buried what they felt was an object used in an unsolved murder. It was put back after it was found. Visitors have gotten EVPS at the altar. It's near the camper. Sonny has placed a device on the altar when I have been in the camper, and we have sat and listened for sounds through wireless headsets. We have heard low voices and movement around it. When we look outside nothing has been there. Since there are deer in the area we try to determine if what we hear are animals.

The slaughterhouse

This was a barn of sorts. It had a loft. The person I interviewed talked about hanging out in the barn. Then along comes the Estes; and they find baby food jars filled with something unknown.

More on the mountain

There have been rumors for years that Sam Bass hid his gold in a cave on this mountain. Kathy and Donna were able to find documentation that showed they could have been friend. This when previous owner, Mr. Yeager was a Texas Ranger. There is also the story of a jewel thief whom robbed a jewelry store. It is slid he came to this mountain to hide his cache. The legend goes that while he was putting his stash deep into a crevice, he managed to knock loose a large boulder. Then that boulder and another rolled over the crevice and sealing the thief inside to never get out. Makes you wonder if his body is still in the crevice. There may be gold in them thar hills.

Then there's the case of a worker on the steep roof. It is said he slipped and fell off the roof dead. So that is a count of three dead outside for sure. What looks like a gravestone was recently found by Sonny while he was clearing a trail up the mountain. The date on the stone is 1901. There's at least one more stone up there that might be another grave marker. Donna is researching the name. Maybe it's a past owner.

Inside the house

There are 12 rooms downstairs and four rooms and a crawl space upstairs. Then there are two rooms outside for a grand total of 18 spaces where activity has occurred. No place is safe even though some spaces seem safer than others once inside the house. I'll start from the back of the house. This is where everyone comes into the house. Parking is in the back.

Pricilla's Room

This is the newest addition. It was the screened in porch. A bathroom was also added to the room. People, even entire paranormal teams, have stayed in this room. They think it's a safe space. Maybe, maybe not. A woman has been seen in the room. She will walk into the wall that is by the Shadowman Room. Sonny and Ryan have seen a cowboy in the room. The figure was in the bathroom and walked into the wall leading into the house. Maybe there was a door there at one time. There is speculation that the slab floor in this room hides an entrance to the hidden basement.

Jacob's Room

It's off the storefront as you enter the house. The room has interesting vibes. I can feel it as soon as I walk into it. The big window has old bars on the inside. They are definitely meant to keep someone in as they are so tightly secured it would be very difficult and time consuming to have them removed. This is the room where a lady was yanked off the bed while Kathy was in there with a group. She was conducting the history part of a tour you can get when you book the house for a night. There was a young couple with the group. They claimed to be Satanist and had a myriad of tattoos fitting their description. When the group went into the room she decided to sit on the bed and lean against the headboard. Soon she was yanked off the bed by an unseen force. It startled everyone and scared her. The video of it has been seen on a number of websites and was shown on Paranormal De-classified. This upset her boyfriend and he returned to the room a few minutes later and yelled at whatever force jerked her off the bed. He was slammed into a wall. By the time they left the next morning they asked Kathy to pray over them and their vehicle. They went from non-believers of God to believers. This has happened at least a half dozen times I know about. Kathy and Sonny were sleeping in the room one night. Kathy woke to find her hair twisted around the bed post. They Estes' believe this is the room Deborah Rentfro stayed in while she lived in the house with her sister. It's also believed abortions may have occurred in this room during the time the house was a brothel. It's also believed many of the abortions may have been against the will of the women stuck in the house as prostitutes. Some of this information has come from spirits speaking in the house. The spirits are quite vocal.

One night when Maria and I were at the house there had been an event. Sonny was the last one to leave the house. Natalie Jones and several cast members of the newest Ghost Hunters were there. They had plans to stay the night after everyone left. Only their plans changed, and they had to leave. Sony had gone inside to make the house was locked, lights were off and so on. When he came out of the house, he got a notification from the security equipment. There is a small casket set up on a table in the living room. There were flowers on top of it and a rosary hung off the top to the side. It was secured in place by the flowers. There is nothing on inside, no windows open and no breeze. The rosary began to swing until it and the flowers on top were pulled off the casket. After that happened the door to Jacob's room opened and, on the video, when you look at the mirror on the far side of the room a face pops up and then the door closes.

The living room

Things happen in here, but it seems not as often. Many people feel somewhat safe and entire groups of people will sleep in here instead of using the bedrooms. A number of rooms are off this room. The piano is in here. A number of people have heard the keys make sounds. It's almost as if a trickster stands nearby and enjoys hitting a key when someone walks by it. Shadows are seen in here. One night when I was there, I watched the camera the next morning to see something odd. One of the visitors was sleeping on the couch by the Scratcher room. While sleeping he removed his knit cap and held it up and behind him. It looked like he was trying to give it to somebody. Then he put it in his lap, sat up, opened his eyes really big and looked around. He was still sleeping. Then he leaned back with his eyes closed. We had to show him the video in the morning. He didn't believe those were his actions when he was told what happened.

The main bathroom by the piano

Not a lot happens here but when it does… There is a curtain that hangs at the entrance. This was placed there because the door tends to open on its own when someone is inside sitting on the toilet. The top shelf of the cabinet will fly open on its own when someone is inside. This has unnerved a few people.

The Shadowman Room

You go through a passage where there may have been a door to outside in the past. The house has several add-ons, and some don't seem to make sense. It butts up against the closet in the Shadowman Room. The closet is creepy. It almost feels like it could be the entrance to the basement. I don't like the closet and I don't know why. One time the tour was in here a male was standing by the closet door. Suddenly he was on the ground writhing in pain. Something had hit him and twisted or punched his jewels. He was in pain for a while. He had also been grabbed there when he was in the Scratcher Room. I have slept in this room a few times. I felt uncomfortable but couldn't put my finger on why. When I stayed the bathroom off of it was still sealed shut.

The Sealed Up Bathroom

The bathroom off the Shadowman Room was sealed shut about 50 years earlier. The only was in was through the window and from the outside. The person I interviewed claimed she and some of her siblings were forced to climb inside and stay there for punishment. She said they would see ghosts and hear voices. Initially that's how Sonny and Kathy entered the room. Since then the bathroom, was unsealed and restored. The bathtub is original as is the medicine chest. The original toilet tank is sitting in the closet in the bedroom. There is a bullet hole in it. The story of what happened is that Priscilla shot a man in there and then turned the gun on herself. There is a photograph of a woman in a blue dress someone took. It is believed this is Priscilla. At one point there looked like something that could have been brain matter and hair was stuck in the corner of the wall by where the toilet had been. Unfortunately, no one will know for sure. Somebody visiting the house decided to scrape it off and take it with them. When the bathroom was getting renovated and an opening was initially cut an EVP was captured on the security camera. It said, "They let Billy out." Any number of people have tried to conduct EVP sessions while sitting in the bathtub. Most of them come out of the tub with scratches.

The Portal Closet

This is a closet off the living room and under the stairs. It seems like a portal area and is in the middle of the house. There is a large mirror inside and visitors like to take pictures of themselves with the mirror in the background. Many feel uneasy with their back to the stairs. I feel that and I don't know why. Visitors have seen faces in their phots with the mirror. Some hear voices inside while others get touched. One individual had their chair lift off the floor. Another person who was there on New Year's Eve got pushed out of the closet. It scared him. He was an atheist and is now a believer in God. Some of the interactions are so scary or violent that it makes believers out of non-believers. This is an unexpected reason for someone to become a Christian. Who would have thought a haunted house would cause someone to suddenly believe in God. Yet it happens. God works in mysterious ways.

The Passage Room

This is the hallway between the Axe Room bathroom and the Scratcher Room. There is a storage room off this room. It was a porch at one time and there are plans to open it up and use the space as a museum for many of the haunted items in the house. If you listen carefully, you can hear footsteps in there. The Passage Room makes any number of people sick to their stomach. It could be from some of the items placed in there. There is an antique doll in a box. There are a bunch of doll clothes not for the doll but have blood on them. This was an actual doll with clothes used in Voodoo ceremonies. According to the person who sold the box to Kathy. There is another Voodoo doll she keeps in the storeroom because of the havoc caused by it. Scratches appeared on the floor by the doll. EVPS in the room have said a number of times Bael is there. This has been recorded on a variety of equipment. Many guests in the home won't go into this room.

The Scratcher Room

This room is different than any room in the house. It appears to have a false wall. It was the bedroom for a male who lived in the house during the time the person I interviewed lived in the house. I can't imagine living in that room. The room got its name because so many people have been scratched in it. I have seen scratches appear on guests. I have been at the table when it has moved and even lifted up. I have been standing there only to hear and feel a chair getting moved. A lot of EVPS are gathered in this room. The walls seem to have space behind them, and the fireplace was never real. I was there one day when Kathy and Donna were digging in the base of the fireplace. Kathy is determined to find the basement. The deeper they dug the more the air in the room seemed to change. There were 4-5 people in the room. Suddenly we all felt pounding coming from below the room. It was as if someone was standing below with a broom handle and knocking it on their ceiling to make the noise stop. The whole floor was vibrating.

The Kitchen

This is the command center for the house and the food center. All the cameras can be seen in here. There are over 20 cameras and there are more that don't show up on the screens. There are cameras in every room, some hallways and on the outside of the house. Some people thinking the kitchen is the safe place will sit in here and watch the cameras all night. A lot of people have even slept on the floor under the large table. Things do happen in here. A few people sleeping on the floor have been grabbed are received bites or scratches. Items have flown off the counters or out of the cabinets. If you are quiet and sit so you can see the stairs and hall you can often see shadows imprint on the curtain hanging in the doorway. You may see shadows pass by and it's not unusual to see light fly by the door.

The Carousel Room

The room got its name because of the toy carousel in there. There are plenty of other toys in the room. Dolls hang from the rafters. The huge fireplace is a fake fireplace. There are openings in the wall going up to the second floor Bottles were found in some of the cubby holes. Some people see a white faced something if they sit in the fireplace in the dark. There used to be an opening on the second floor and some of the children of previous owners used the cubby holes to climb and sneak upstairs. The girl I interviewed said their dog was upstairs and fell to its death down the open chimney hole. The Estes' have the hole covered upstairs so no one can fall down it. A lot of EVPS are picked up in this room. Sometimes some of the dolls with randomly begin to swing. There is no breeze in that room. The window unit AC doesn't blow hard enough to swing the dolls. It happens as well when no AC or heater is on. The carousel used to light up on its own when it was turned off. Odd things would happen if it was moved. There was a play phone in the hall that kept going off one night. It kept ringing and the people staying that night thought it had to be a trick phone. That is until they were shown the next morning it was a toy and there was nothing attached that could make it ring.

The Axe Room

This is the room by the stairs and front door. It's one you either want to stay in or you don't. I like it. Many people won't stay in it due to the activity. That's why I stay in it. You can hear footsteps going up and down the stairs all night. You can hear the walking upstairs from this room. I have been in it and heard the sounds of people gathered in the living room. You can hear a multitude of voices but not quite be able to make out what is being said. This is the room where I have gotten growled or hissed at a few times. Not too long ago I was in here laying down. I didn't feel well when I had been fine. I was laying on the far side of the bed with my eyes closed. I must have head at least six times a hiss. Each time it was louder. I ignored it. One of the times it was loud enough people in the Scratcher Room heard it when I did. I clearly heard a disembodied voice about six time as well. It kept saying in that scratchy Toby voice to "Get out." I ignored it as well.

Upstairs Toby's Room and the Moonshine Room

Toby's room connects to the Moonshine room. Toby's room is unsettling, and a lot of people run out of this room screaming, even falling on the stairs they are in such a rush to get downstairs. People feel Toby. They have gotten pictures of him, and they hear, get out, a lot. The Moonshine room is fairly tame most of the time. Musical instruments have been heard in there. There have been many growls heard in Toby's room. Glowing eyes have been captured in this room as have many EVPs. If using an SLS camera an image of something is often seen on either side of the door inside this room. Someone once captured an amazing photograph with their Go Pro camera. They snapped a quick picture. In the picture something ugly and green with glowing eyes was peeking out of an opening. It is thought this is Toby.

Joshua's Room

There are toys in here. People try to communicate with the boy who was murdered upstairs by being beat. It is said he died in a corner of the attic while hiding. There are balls in this room and in Toby's room. I have awakened when in the Axe room only to find balls from upstairs at the bottom of the stairs when no one had been up there. A favorite spot for people is through the door in Joshua's room. It leads to the attic. There are toys and balls for Joshua in there. One time a group was back there when a ball came rolling down the area by the door and into where they were sitting. No one had rolled the ball. Often toys are moved around at night. I have gone into Joshua's room and sat in the chair by the wall to the attic while wearing bionic ears. One time during the day I was in the house alone. There were workers outside doing something to the house. I heard something I had not heard before and it felt new to the house. I heard boots walking back and forth, almost stomping. It didn't sound friendly. In fat, the longer I listened the more agitated the steps sounded. I decided to go and see if it could have been one of the workers. It wasn't. They weren't even on that side of the house. There is a child's blow-up punching bag on the back wall. We have watched through the monitors a shadow cross the room toward the tall punching bag. We watched as the bag would rock back and forth as if a child was playing with it.

Emily's Room

I think this is one of the most active rooms in the house. I like to sit with my back to the wall where I can see the hall. The name didn't come from a dead spirit. So many EVPS, growls, hisses and audible voices have happened in this room. There's a mirror in here that seems like a portal. People have been touched in here.

IN CLOSING

T here are many things that happen in the house. The security cameras record many EVPS when no one is in the house. Some people have come here to speak to loved ones passed on. They believe they recognize the voices. EVPS captured here have foretold of future events. They even mentioned the pandemic. This is why there is too much to put in one book and the series was born. This will allow me to go in depth about EVPS, spirits, murders and so much more.

The stories, myths and history of the house seem to find themselves mired in legends yet steeped in documented detail. The wells of the house have long been hidden but that may change one day. Were there children kidnapped by the Native Americans a long time ago? Was there one who got away or was released and was a movie made based loosely on the events? Are there tunnels or caves? Did Sam Bass hide his gold nearby? What happened to the jewel thief whom may have died on the mountain? Is he still there covered by a boulder or two? Where did he hide the stolen jewelry? What relative of one of the landowners whom shot his father in California? What about the basement and the old barn? What about the brothel or the make-shift hospital? So much to digest that it nearly seems impossible.

I welcome input from this book. If you have information regarding the house, especially historical information or photographs of the house I would love to see them. If you have any information about the lot next door, it would be fantastic. We know it was a yellow house the city tore down. Through people living in Mineral Wells and a few who have been in the house it was identified at one point to be a drug house where murders occurred.

There is an unsolved murder where the person who went missing for a year was last seen at this house. She knew the people who lived there and would hang out at the house. There is quite a bit of speculation as to how she died. There is also speculation about another murder. This one had a male confess to the murder. He is in prison and refuses to say where he buried the body. Someone who used to live in the house told me and told Kathy that she was chopped up and put into three boxes. She said she may be buried on HHH property. All this is being researched and people are being interviewed. They are mysteries we hope to solve to give the victims' families peace and closure.

Now for a few photos, historical and paranormal...

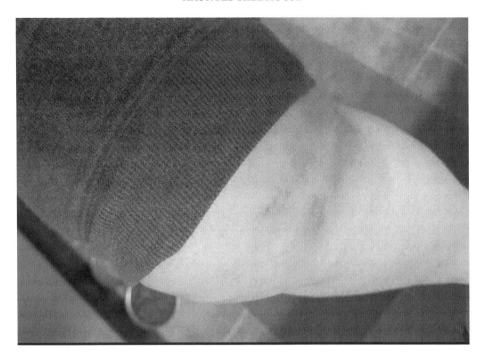

This person was resting in the Axe Room when she woke up, she found this bruise on her leg.

Another person scratched

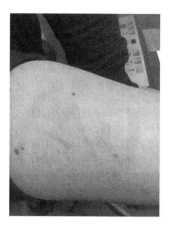

Another person scratched

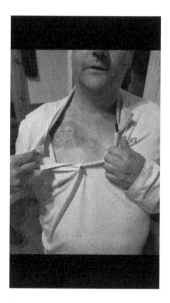

Below a light anomaly in Joshua's room.

S oon after Judge Lynch came to town he ordered all the wells to be sealed. This is when a part of HHH was built over one of the wells. This photograph was used on the cover of Time Was In Mineral Wells written by A.F. Weaver. This photograph was taken on East Mountain.

J. A. LYNCH, FOUNDER OF MINERAL WELLS

Judge J. A. Lynch (1827-1920) founder of Mineral Wells.
From a painting by Thomas Beauregard and owned by
Julia Lynch Hargett, granddaughter of Judge and Mrs. Lynch.

The Opening of the First Season at Mineral Wells, Artwork, n.d.; digital image,
(http://texashistory.unt.edu/ark:/67531/metapth20224/ : accessed June 09, 2014), University of North
Texas Libraries, The Portal to Texas History, http://texashistory.unt.edu; crediting Boyce Ditto Public

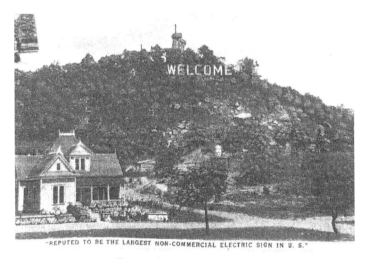

"REPUTED TO BE THE LARGEST NON-COMMERCIAL ELECTRIC SIGN IN U. S."

Welcome Sign & Lookout Tower 1929

TEXAS STATE BOARD OF HEALTH
Bureau of Vital Statistics

STANDARD CERTIFICATE OF DEATH

No. 16,934

Reg. No. A.X.X.

2499

PLACE OF DEATH

County Palo Pinto

City Mineral Wells   (Su............... St;............... Ward;...............)   [If death occurred in a hospital or institution, give its NAME instead of street and number.]

2 FULL NAME   Fannie Yeager Nylee

PERSONAL AND STATISTICAL PARTICULARS   MEDICAL PARTICULARS

3 SEX   4 Color or Race   5 Single, Married, Widowed, or Divorced (If write the word) | 16 DATE OF DEATH   July   22   1924
Female   white   Widowed | (Month)   (Day)   (Year)

| 17 I HEREBY CERTIFY, That I attended deceased from

6 DATE OF BIRTH   June   13   1839 | 191... to ...2..2..4.. 191...
(Month)   (Day)   (Year) | that I last saw h.er. alive on 7.2.2.4 191...
7 AGE   85   yrs.   1   mos.   9   ds. | and that death occurred, on the date stated above, at 11.30 ..m
If less than 2 years state if less than 1 day | The CAUSE OF DEATH* was as follows:
Yes.......... No..........   hrs.......... mins.......... | Enlargement of Prostate

8 OCCUPATION |
(a) Trade, profession or particular kind of work | (Duration)   yrs.   mos.   ds.
(b) General nature of industry, business, or establishment in which employed (or employer) | Contributory
| (Secondary)   (Duration)   yrs.   mos.   ds.
9 BIRTHPLACE   Tennessee | (Signed)   F. L. Yeagor   M. D.
(State or country) | 7/23/24   191...   (Address) Mineral Wells

10 NAME OF FATHER   Cornelius F. Yeager | * State the DISEASE CAUSING DEATH, or in deaths from VIOLENT CAUSES, state (1) MEANS OF INJURY; and (2) whether ACCIDENTAL, SUICIDAL, or HOMICIDAL.

11 BIRTHPLACE OF FATHER   Tennessee | 18 LENGTH OF RESIDENCE (For Hospitals, Institutions, Transients, or Recent Residents)
(State or country) | At place   yrs.   mos.   ds.   In the
12 MAIDEN NAME OF MOTHER   Selina Sloan | of death   State   yrs.   mos.   ds.
| Where was disease contracted,
13 BIRTHPLACE OF MOTHER   Tennessee | if not at place of death?
(State or country) | Former or usual residence

14 THE ABOVE IS TRUE TO THE BEST OF MY KNOWLEDGE | 19 PLACE OF BURIAL OR REMOVAL   DATE OF BURIAL
(Informant) Mrs. L. D. Brattin | Elmwood Cemetery   July 23 1924
(Address) Mineral Wells | 20 UNDERTAKER   ADDRESS
15 Filed   7-24-24 J. H. McBracken   Registrar | A. H. Betham   Mineral Wells

WRITE PLAINLY WITH UNFADING INK—THIS IS A PERMANENT RECORD.

WELL—INSTRUCTIONS ON THE REVERSE SIDE.

Where Stillborn is given as cause of death, file birth certificate. Every item of information should be care fully supplied. AGE should be stated EXACTLY. PHYSICIANS should state CAUSE OF DEATH in plain terms, so that it may be properly classified. Exact statement of OCCUPATION is very important.

Mountain View, Mineral Wells, Texas

112

FAT MAN'S REDUCER UP EAST MOUNTAIN
Built in 1905, these some 1,000 steps went up
the mountain from N. E. 3rd Street and were
torn down around the 1940's.

OPENING OF THE FIRST SEASON AT MINERAL WELLS

Some of the photographs used in this book were given to me by
Kathy Estes.
Some were given to Kathy by Phil Kirckhoff
Some were obtained through historical documents
Some were obtained through Find A Grave
Some were listed in Time Was in Mineral Wells by A.F. Weaver

Shadowman seen looking through the door of the old camper

Here is a photograph of the real Toby that has never been published before, in book form or on television.

ABOUT THE AUTHOR

Martha Hazzard Decker

Martha Decker has been involved in investigating the paranormal since 1999 and is the founder of East Texas Paranormal. She was on Portals to Hell and Death Walker. Her experience includes investigating private homes, commercial businesses, historical sites and public locations, UFOs and cryptids. Decker has worked with cities that contacted her regarding activity in municipal buildings. Decker works with law enforcement agencies to help solve unsolved murders. She is an empath and has experience as an investigator, writer, author and photographer. Decker retired in 2007 from law enforcement as assistant chief of police and detective. While in law enforcement Decker was a negotiator, instructor, specialized in domestic terrorism and crimes against children. She worked with federal and State agencies. She worked for the State of Texas as a child death investigator, was a speaker, educator and worked with the anti-human trafficking task force. She's a process server and was a private investigator. Decker experienced a number of unexplained occurrences as a child which triggered her interest into the unknown. She often speaks on how to use common law enforcement techniques and apply them to paranormal interviews and investigations, including how to interview children. Decker's photography has been published in newspapers, magazines and even on the cover of phone books in west Texas. Her book, Paranormal Profiling, was published in 2014. Decker has spent many nights alone at Haunted Hill House researching information for the book. It's been many months in the making and she can't wait for it to become available. In 1995, Decker received a first place award from the Associated Press for specialty reporting while working as a journalist for the Cedar Creek Pilot. Decker writes articles for Medium.com. She has over 20 years of investigative experience ranging from criminal to civil and journalistic. In the mid-eighties she produced and directed several television shows, including Ray Wylie Hubbard Live at Dallas Palace. Decker also spent over 10 years as a volunteer firefighter and rescue SCUBA diver.

Author of Paranormal Profiling, and seen on Portals to Hell and Death Walker.

Want to know more?
Contact her at –
marthadecker.com
easttexasparanormal,com
Twitter - @mardeck
Instagram - @mardeck
TikTok - @marthdecker

Made in the USA
Monee, IL
12 July 2021

72836040R00074